ENGLISH GRAMMAR

Book Four

By the same author
ENGLISH COMPOSITION FOR BEGINNERS
ENGLISH COMPOSITION LESSONS
PRECIS WRITING: MODELS AND METHODS
TEACHING ENGLISH TO BEGINNERS

ENGLISH GRAMMAR AND EXERCISES

Book Four

For Secondary Classes

by L. R. H. CHAPMAN

LONGMAN

LONGMAN GROUP UK LIMITED
Longman House, Burnt Mill, Harlow
Essex CM20 2JE, England
and Associated Companies throughout the world.

© L. R. H. Chapman 1967

All rights reserved; no part of this publication may be reproduced, stored in a retrieval system, or transmitted in any form or by any means, electronic, mechanical, photocopying, recording, or otherwise, without the prior written permission of the Publishers.

First published * 1967
Seventy-eighth impression 1993

Produced by Longman Singapore Publishers Pte Ltd
Printed in Singapore

ISBN 0-582-52069-X

Contents

1. The Verb – Revision ... 1
   Observation 1 ... 6
2. The Perfect Tenses ... 8
   Observation 2 ... 21
3. The Passive ... 23
   Observation 3 ... 30
4. The Continuous Tenses ... 32
   Observation 4 ... 45
5. One Future Tense Only ... 48
   Observation 5 ... 52
6. Conditional Tenses ... 54
   Observation 6 ... 67
7. Should have + Part 3 and Similar Verb Forms ... 69
   Observation 7 ... 77
8. Have to ... 79
   Observation 8 ... 88
9. Be able to ... 90
   Observation 9 ... 96
10. Past Forms, but not Past Time ... 98
    Observation 10 ... 110
11. Verb-Nouns ... 113
    Observation 11 ... 125

To the Teacher

This book is intended for secondary classes which have previously worked through Books 1–3 of this series. The exercises are more numerous and longer, to suit the larger needs of secondary pupils, and the vocabulary is naturally wider, although remaining within the limits of everyday educated use. As in Books 1–3, the exercises have been framed so that the average pupil CAN do them and NOT make mistakes, if he keeps to the paths laid down for him.

The exercises should be done orally, to the extent that time permits; but the importance of writing, to 'fix' knowledge, perhaps needs to be emphasised. Writing makes 'an exact man', as the essayist Bacon wrote over three hundred years ago, and today it is still true.

L. R. H. C.

1 The Verb – Revision

1 English verbs, except a few which are defective, are 'full' or complete verbs, that is, they have 3 parts. These parts are called in grammar (1) the stem, (2) the past tense, and (3) the past participle.

It is usual to learn irregular verbs by their 3 parts, for example: begin-began-begun, do-did-done, have-had-had, tell-told-told, cut-cut-cut. There is one irregular verb which has two forms of Part 2, the past tense: be-was, were-been.

Part 2 and Part 3 of regular verbs are made in the SAME way, by adding -ed or -d to Part 1, for example: walk-walked-walked, play-played-played, like-liked-liked, hope-hoped-hoped.

The stem and the past participle are used in a number of ways for making different tenses and forms of verbs, and we think it will help the student if they are called Part 1 and Part 3, or simply 1 and 3, and not by their grammatical names.

2 There are two uses of Part 1 which need a lot of practice:

A

> I WORK fairly hard, but my father WORKS much harder.
> My brother and I GO to the cinema occasionally, but my sister GOES once a week.

The verbs in these sentences are in the present tense. This tense is 1, and in the 3rd Person singular 1 + s, or 1 + es. There are two exceptions: the present tense of the verb be-was, were-been, and the 3rd Person singular *has* of the verb have-had-had.

Exercise 1

Say, or write, the following sentences again, beginning with the Subject (3rd Person singular) in brackets:

Example: Some people begin work very early in the morning. (A postman)

Lesson 1

Answer : A postman BEGINS work very early in the morning.

1. I have breakfast at half past seven. (My father)
2. We make mistakes sometimes. (A pupil)
3. I never wear a hat in the summer. (My brother)
4. Most of my friends play football. (My best friend)
5. I do my homework before supper. (My sister)
6. I sit at the back of the class. (Jack)
7. We sometimes forget the time. (My mother)
8. I'm nearly sixteen. (My cousin)
9. A lot of English boys have fair hair. (My English friend)
10. Some people get up very late. (My neighbour)
11. I watch television every evening. (My father)
12. Women like to look at the shop windows. (My sister)
13. I have a hot bath twice a week. (She)
14. We finish the day's work at six o'clock. (The clerk)
15. Some people do nothing during the holidays. (He)
16. I am never late. (The teacher)
17. Mr. and Mrs. Brown usually go to bed before midnight. (Mr. Brown)
18. Those children help their mother. (The little girl)
19. I spend a lot of money on books. (The teacher)
20. A lot of Arabs speak English. (Ahmad)
21. They prefer coffee to tea. (He)
22. I get up at seven every morning. (My father)
23. We like to go for a walk in the evening. (The old man)
24. I sometimes buy a packet of biscuits. (My mother)
25. The servants sweep the floors every morning. (The servant)

B

Q. Do you and your brother often GO to the cinema?

A. No, I don't GO very often, and my brother doesn't GO unless there's a good film. He went last week, but I didn't GO with him. I was busy and couldn't GO. There's a good film on next week, and I may GO to see it, but I won't GO unless my brother comes with me.

In these sentences the verb *go* occurs seven times, and in *each* case it is Part 1 of the verb. One of the most important rules of English is:

> Helping verbs (see Book 2, Lesson 23) are used with Part 1, the form of which NEVER changes. In the above sentences, it is ALWAYS *go*.

Exercise 2

Complete the following sentences with negative verbs. Then ask and answer shortly 2 questions about each sentence, as in these examples:

Example 1: He writes very quickly, but he ——— clearly.

Answer : He writes very quickly, but he doesn't WRITE clearly.
Does he WRITE very quickly? Yes, he does.
Does he WRITE clearly? No, he doesn't.

Example 2: I kept the letter, but I ——— the envelope.

Answer : I kept the letter, but I didn't KEEP the envelope.
Did you KEEP the letter? Yes, I did.
Did you KEEP the envelope? No, I didn't.

Note: The verbs *write* and *keep* printed in capitals in the above examples are Part 1.

1 He gets up early on weekdays, but he ——— up early on Sundays.
2 Mr. Smith teaches English, but he ——— other subjects.
3 I flew from Cairo to Beirut, but I ——— back.
4 She drinks a lot of tea, but she ——— much coffee.
5 They sat in the garden, but they ——— there for long.
6 I understood the first question, but I ——— the others.
7 They work hard, but they ——— more than seven hours a day.
8 He grew a lot of flowers in his garden, but he ——— roses.
9 I bought a raincoat, but I ——— an umbrella.
10 He spends a lot of money, but he ——— all his salary.

11 We like fish, but we ——— to eat it every day.

12 Jack learnt French at school, but he ——— German.

13 He wrote to my father, but he ——— to me.

14 She buys a lot of food every day, but she ——— much meat.

15 I won a prize, but I ——— the first prize.

16 He lost money at the races, but he ——— much.

17 They walk to school, but they ——— home.

18 English people eat a lot of potatoes, but they ——— much rice.

19 I went to the seaside last weekend, but I ——— by car.

20 The bell rang at the beginning of the lesson, but it ——— at the end.

21 He does homework every evening, but he ——— much.

22 I made a mistake, but I ——— a bad one.

23 She plays the piano, but she ——— it very well.

24 I saw Ahmad yesterday, but I ——— him the day before yesterday.

25 It rained very hard, but it ——— all night.

26 I know Yusef, but I ——— his brother.

27 He smokes a lot, but he ——— before breakfast.

28 That shop sells office furniture, but it ——— typewriters.

29 The police caught one of the thieves, but they ——— the other.

30 She sent a telegram, but she ——— it to the right address.

31 He sold his house, but he ——— his furniture.

32 I felt tired, but I ——— unwell.

33 The little girl goes to school, but she ——— in the afternoons.

34 His father gives him pocket-money, but he ——— him much.

35 She found her bag, but she ——— her purse.

3 Two very important uses of Part 3 of the verb are as follows:

A

1 Most teachers are PAID monthly.

2 He was KILLED in a railway accident.

3 The doctor told Mrs. Smith, "Don't worry. Your child will be TAKEN good care of in hospital."
4 A baby cannot feed itself; it must be FED.
5 This letter is important. It should be ANSWERED at once.

The words printed in capitals are Part 3 of the verbs pay, kill, take, feed, and answer. They are used with different tenses or parts of the verb *be* to make the passive form.

Exercise 3

Put the verbs in brackets in the correct passive form. Choose the right tense.

1 The bell (ring) at the beginning of each lesson.
2 A lot of ships (sink) by submarines in the last war.
3 The thieves are still free, but I think they (catch) soon.
4 That tree (strike) by lightning a year ago.
5 The word *beginning* (spell) with a double n.
6 I played a very good game of tennis, but I (beat).
7 The lost child (find) last night fast asleep under a tree.
8 A foreign language can't (learn) in a few weeks.
9 He works very hard; I'm sure he (give) a rise in salary next year.
10 These are very good shoes; they (make) of the best leather.
11 It was a terrible fire. The house (burn) to the ground, and four people (burn) to death.
12 Ahmad said, "I hope I (meet) when I arrive at London Airport."
13 I don't like to (tell) I'm a fool.
14 Letters to foreign countries (send) usually by airmail.
15 In hot weather meat must (keep) in a cool place.
16 The carpenter said, "The work (not finish) until next week."
17 He's a very rude boy; he should (teach) good manners.
18 You (bite) if you go near that dog.
19 The news can (hear) on the wireless at 6 p.m.
20 He died a long time ago, but his work (not forget) yet.

B

1. Have you ever BEEN to America?
2. I haven't SEEN my eldest brother since 1963.
3. The doctor isn't at home; he has just GONE out.
4. The land is very dry; it hasn't RAINED for two months.
5. The maid denied that she had STOLEN the money.
6. He told me that he hadn't RIDDEN a bicycle since he was a little boy.

The words printed in capitals are Part 3 of the verbs *be, see, go, rain, steal,* and *ride.* The verbs of which these words are a part are in the Perfect tense. In sentences 1–4 they are in the Present Perfect tense; in sentences 5 and 6 they are in the Past Perfect tense.

Perfect tenses, which will be dealt with more fully in the next chapter, are made with any tense or form of the verb *have* + Part 3.

Observation 1

Note to the teacher: A language exercise has a main purpose: to give practice in *one* point of grammar, but it must contain a number of other useful linguistic points, such as the correct use of prepositions, adverb particles, conjunctions, and other parts of speech; whether it is right or wrong to use the Articles *a* and *the*; the right choice of words which pupils often confuse; whether Singular or Plural forms should be used, etc. Such linguistic points (to which correct spelling can be added) can be learnt by observation, and the purpose of the exercises which follow each chapter is to train the pupils' powers of observation. The exercises consist of sentences taken from the preceding chapter: they are suitable for oral work in class, preferably after home preparation, during which pupils should check their answers by looking back at the sentences in the preceding chapter.

Sentences from Exercises 1, 2, or 3 of Chapter 1

Which is the correct preposition to put in each space: *at, by, in, on,* or *to*?

1. I spend a lot of money – books.

The Verb – Revision 7

2 I sit – the back of the class.
3 Jack learnt French – school, but he didn't learn German.
4 I went to the seaside last weekend, but I didn't go – car.
5 A foreign language can't be learnt – a few weeks.
6 Ahmad said, "I hope I'll be met when I arrive – London Airport."
7 He gets up early – weekdays, but he doesn't get up early – Sundays.
8 The bell rang – the beginning of the lesson, but it didn't ring – the end.
9 The news can be heard – the wireless – 6 p.m.
10 They prefer coffee – tea.
11 The little girl goes – school, but she doesn't go – the afternoons.
12 Letters to foreign countries are usually sent – airmail.
13 We like to go for a walk – the evening.
14 It was a terrible fire. The house was burnt – the ground, and four people were burnt – death.

Choose the correct word from those in brackets.

(a) **Singular or Plural?**

1 A lot of English boys have fair (hair, hairs).
2 Mr. Smith teaches English, but he doesn't teach other (subject, subjects).
3 He sold his house, but he didn't sell his (furniture, furnitures).
4 He's a very rude boy; he should be taught good (manner, manners).
5 The police caught one of the thieves, but (he, they) didn't catch the other.

(b) **The verb *do* or the verb *make*?**

1 We (do, make) mistakes sometimes.
2 Some people (do, make) nothing during the holidays.
3 I (do, make) my homework before supper.

2 The Perfect Tenses

1 The Present Perfect tense: have, has + Part 3

We learnt in Book 3 that this tense is used

(1) to describe a past action or happening when our mind is on the PRESENT result or effect, as in these sentences:

> I've read most of Shakespeare's plays.
> The bell has just rung.

(2) to speak about a period of time which began in the past and continues until the PRESENT, as in these sentences:

> His shirt is very dirty; he has worn it for nearly a week.
> She hasn't bought a new pair of shoes since 1962.

(3) to speak about a period of time which now, in the PRESENT, is not yet finished, as in these sentences:

> Today is October 25th; I've done very little work this month.
> I listened to the Minister's broadcast last night, and I've never in my life heard such a good speech.

The word *present* has been printed in capitals above to emphasise that this tense is really a PRESENT tense; when we use it, we are looking back to, or remembering, the past. Perhaps a better name for the tense would be the Present-Past. The difference between this tense and the past tense can be seen from the following sentences:

> I've read this book several times. I first read it in 1960.

In the first sentence, the speaker uses the Present Perfect tense because he has the PRESENT knowledge or memory of reading this book. In the second sentence, he uses the Past tense because 1960 is finished, 'dead', and not connected with the present.

> He hasn't had a holiday since 1962, but he had a very long holiday in 1961.

The first verb is in the Present Perfect tense, because 'since 1962' means 'from 1962 until the PRESENT'. The second verb is in the Past tense, because 'in 1961' is in a finished, 'dead' past, not connected with the present.

Exercise 1

Put the verbs in brackets into the Present Perfect OR the Past tense. If there is an adverb in brackets at the end of the sentence, as in Example 1, put it in the right place.

Example 1: I (write) to the manager a fortnight ago, but I've not had a reply, so I (write) again. (JUST)

Answer: I *wrote* to the manager a fortnight ago, but I've not had a reply, so *I've* just *written* again.

Note: The adverb is placed between *have* and Part 3.

Example 2: It's 3 p.m. and he (not eat) anything today, but he (eat) a good dinner last night.

Answer: It's 3 p.m. and he *hasn't eaten* anything today, but he *ate* a good dinner last night.

1. Today is Thursday, and John (be) late twice this week; he (be) late yesterday and on Monday.
2. I first (meet) George a month ago, and I (meet) him several times since then.
3. We're in September now, and we (do) a lot of work this year; we (do) a lot last year also.
4. She (buy) a coat last winter, but she (not buy) a new dress since 1963.
5. It's only the middle of the month, and he (spend) most of his salary; he (spend) £15 yesterday. (ALREADY)
6. I (break) my leg in 1960, but I (break) my arm. (NEVER)
7. He's over sixty, and he's still working. He (work) hard all his life. When he was a young man, he sometimes (work) all night.
8. The postman (come) at eight yesterday, but it's now half past eight and he (not come) yet.
9. Today is April 23rd. Mary (not be) absent this month, but she (be) absent for three days in March.
10. He (feel) extremely ill when he went to hospital, but he (feel) much better since he came out of hospital a month ago.
11. It's only 11 a.m. and he (smoke) twenty cigarettes; he (smoke) three or four before breakfast. (ALREADY)
12. It (rain) very heavily last Monday, but it (not rain) much since then.

13 She (not take) her little boy to a theatre yet, but she (take) him to a cinema for the first time a few days ago.

14 Henry (play) football at school, but he (not play) since he left school in 1963.

15 The headmistress (speak) to Mary about her work at the beginning of the school year, but she (not speak) again since then.

16 It's eight o'clock, and the baby (wake) up; it (wake) up much earlier yesterday morning. (JUST)

17 He (give) his daughter £1000 when she got married in 1961, but he (not give) her any money since then.

18 The author is still a young man. He (write) his last book in 1960, but he (not write) anything since then.

19 I (fly) non-stop from London to Cairo, but I (fly) non-stop from Rome in September 1963. (NEVER)

20 Mr. Jones (drink) a lot of coffee when he was working in the Middle East, but he (not drink) much since he came back to England.

21 She's going to be married next month. She (choose) her wedding dress yesterday, but she (not choose) any other clothes yet.

22 This dog is dangerous. It (bite) several people; it (bite) the postman badly yesterday morning. (ALREADY)

23 The police (catch) two of the escaped prisoners last night, but they (not catch) the third yet.

24 He borrowed £10 three months ago. He (pay) back half of it last month, but he (not pay) back the other £5 yet.

2 The Past Perfect tense: had + Part 3

We have already learnt that this tense is used in Indirect Speech when the Present Perfect or the Past tense is used in Direct Speech, for example:

> Mary said, "I *haven't done* my homework."
> Mary said (that) she *hadn't done* her homework.
>
> The policeman asked me, "*Did* you *see* the accident?"
> The policeman asked me if I *had seen* the accident.

If we examine these sentences, we shall find a reason for using the Past Perfect tense.

When did Mary say her sentence? At some time in the past, perhaps to her teacher one morning at school. But she didn't do her homework the evening before. So we have two past times: the past when she spoke, and the earlier past, which is sometimes called the before-past, when she didn't do her homework.

When did the policeman ask me his question? At some time in the past. When did the accident happen? In an earlier past, or a before-past, *before* he asked the question. Again, we have two past times, one further from the present than the other.

The Past Perfect tense is therefore used to join grammatically two past actions or happenings, one of which took place in the before-past, that is, in an earlier past than the other.

Study these sentences:

> The sick man felt better (in the evening).
> He took his medicine (in the afternoon).

First, the sick man took his medicine. He felt better later. The evening was in the past; the afternoon was in the before-past. The sentences can be joined:

> The sick man felt better *after* he *had taken* his medicine.

The joining word is *after*, followed by a Past Perfect tense.

> We reached the station (at five past nine).
> The train left (at nine).

The train left. Five minutes later, we reached the station. Five past nine was a past time; nine was before-past. The sentences can be joined:

> *When* we reached the station, the train *had left*.
> or
> The train *had left when* we reached the station.

The joining word is *when*, but notice that it is followed by a Past tense *reached*. The Past Perfect tense *had left* is used in the principal part of the sentence.

Lesson 2

Consider now these sentences:

> The postman came (at 8 o'clock).
> I finished breakfast (at ten past eight).

Here we have two happenings in the past that follow one another. The Past Perfect tense can be used to join them grammatically:

> When the postman came, I *had* not *finished* breakfast.
> or
> The postman came (ten minutes) before I *had finished* breakfast.

Note that the joining word *before* is followed by the Past Perfect tense.

Exercise 2

Put the verbs in brackets into the Past OR Past Perfect tense:

1. The new bus-driver (have) an accident after he (drive) a few yards.
2. He foolishly (buy) a new car before he (sell) his old one.
3. When I (get) to the cinema, the film (start).
4. Yusef (leave) school when his father (die).
5. The pupils (enter) the classroom five minutes before the bell (ring).
6. After she (lock) and (bolt) all the doors, she (go) to bed.
7. The pupils (do) the exercise very well after the teacher (show) them how to.
8. Mary (go) home when her mother (get) to the school.
9. He (begin) to answer my question before I (finish) asking it.
10. The thief (hide) the money when the police (come) to search his room.
11. The little boy (tell) a lie five minutes after he (promise) to tell the truth.
12. I (wake) up this morning half an hour before the sun (rise).
13. When the plane (land), the sun (set).
14. She (feel) sick after she (eat) a whole box of chocolates.
15. After the doctor (examine) the child he (have) a talk with the mother.
16. He (buy) a typewriter long before he (learn) how to type.
17. When I (call) on my friend, he (go) out.

18 The miser (feel) happier after he (hide) his money under the floor.
19 The teacher (start) giving a dictation before the pupils (write) the date in their exercise-books.
20 Mary (finish) her homework when her father (come) home from his office.
21 He (jump) off the bus before it (stop).
22 I (throw) away the newspaper after I (read) it.
23 The baby (fell) out of bed when Mrs. Brown (go) into the bedroom.
24 The foolish young man (get) married six months before he (find) a job.
25 After she (spend) all her money she (ask) her father to help her.
26 The thief (break) the shop window when the policeman (see) him.
27 Both her parents (die) before she (finish) her education.
28 The teacher (give) back the exercise-books after he (correct) them.
29 The sun (rise) when the farmer (start) work.
30 One or two pupils (begin) to play and make a noise before the teacher (go) out of the classroom.

Read these sentences:

He walked ten miles. Then he felt tired.

Here again are two past happenings, which followed each other. First, he walked ten miles; *after* walking ten miles, he felt tired. If we wish to emphasise that he did not feel tired during this long walk, we can join the sentences:

He *didn't feel* tired *until* he *had walked* ten miles.

The second happening is put at the beginning of the sentence, the verb is made negative, and *then* is left out. The joining word is *until*, followed by the Past Perfect tense *had walked*.

Exercise 3

Join in the same way the following pairs of sentences. The first pair are joined for you.

Lesson 2

1. Mary finished her homework. Then she went out. Mary didn't go out until she had finished her homework.
2. I read the newspaper from beginning to end. Then I went to bed.
3. The little boy cut his finger badly. Then he stopped playing with his knife.
4. Ahmad learnt French. Then he went to France.
5. She spent all the money in her purse. Then she left the shop.
6. The clock struck nine. Then Jack woke up.
7. The doctor saw all the patients in the hospital. Then he had a rest.
8. He saved £500. Then he got married.
9. The sun set. The farmer stopped work.
10. The nurse gave him two sleeping pills. Then he went to sleep.
11. We answered all the questions. Then we left the examination room.
12. She said Please. Then I gave her a piece of chocolate.
13. The Prime Minister finished his speech. Then I turned off the wireless.
14. The bell rang. Then the pupils entered the classroom.
15. She did all the housework. Then she sat down.
16. He lost all his money. Then he stopped playing cards.
17. The teacher corrected all the compositions. Then he went home.
18. I asked him three times for the money. Then he paid me.

Every sentence in this lesson which contained a Past Perfect tense contained also a Past tense. It is most important to understand that a sentence which contains only a Past Perfect tense, and which stands alone, by itself, has NO meaning. The following sentence, by itself, has NO meaning:

> He *had spent* all his money.

We can give this sentence meaning in the following ways. Notice that in each case a Past tense is added.

1. He *told* me that he *had spent* all his money.

2 He *came* home from his holiday after he *had spent* all his money.

3 He *came* home from his holiday before he *had spent* all his money.

4 When he *came* home from his holiday, he *had spent* all his money.

5 He *didn't come* home from his holiday until he *had spent* all his money.

We can also give the sentence meaning if another sentence or other sentences are put with it, for example:

> It was midnight. The young man stood at the street corner. He didn't know what to do, or where to go. He had spent all his money, and his pockets were empty.

The past time was midnight. At midnight, the young man stood at the street corner. At midnight, he didn't know what to do, or where to go. At midnight, his pockets were empty. But he had spent all his money BEFORE midnight. Past tenses, *was, stood, didn't know, were*, are used for the past time (midnight), and the Past Perfect tense *had spent* is used for the before-past time (before midnight).

Here are other sentences, in which a past time is expressed by using Past tenses, and a before-past time by using Past Perfect tenses:

> It *was* ten p.m. (a past time) and the doctor *felt* very tired (at ten p.m.). He *had got* up early that morning (a before-past time), and *had worked* hard all day (before ten p.m., in the before-past). He *sat* down (at ten p.m.) and *lit* a cigarette (at ten p.m., a past time). He *had eaten* nothing since breakfast (in the before-past time between breakfast and ten p.m.), but he *did not feel* hungry (at ten p.m., a past time).

Exercise 4

Put the verbs between brackets into the Past OR the Past Perfect tense. Notice that a past time is given in the first sentence of each passage, and that a Past tense is used to express this time.

1

The tourists arrived at London Airport early on Monday morning. They (leave) Cairo on Sunday evening. They (spend) a fortnight in Egypt and (see) most of the sights. After they (show) their passports to the official and (pass) through the Customs, they (get) on the BOAC bus and (go) to the Terminal.

2

The examination finished at noon. Jack gave his answer paper to the teacher and (leave) the room. He (not answer) all the questions. He (write) very long answers to three questions, and there (not be) enough time to answer the other two.

3

She came out of the shop just before closing-time. She (look) at more than twenty dresses, but she (not buy) anything. She (be) tired after looking at so many dresses, and she (not go) home until she (have) a cup of tea and a cake in a tea-shop.

4

Henry came home at half past eleven last night. He (meet) a friend in the street at seven o'clock and (go) to the cinema with him. When he got home, the house (be) in darkness. Everybody (go) to bed.

5

Mr. Jones left the hospital at the end of April. He (break) his leg in March and (be) in hospital for about five weeks. He (get) into a taxi and (go) straight home. He (tell) everybody at home that the doctors and nurses (look) after him very well.

6

I saw Mr. Brown yesterday, driving my old car. I (sell) it to him three months before, and he (pay) me half the price. But he still (owe) me £125. When I (see) him in my old car, I (tell) myself that I (do) a foolish thing, selling it to a man like Mr. Brown.

7

The young man got up early on Tuesday morning and (look) out of the window of his hotel bedroom. The sun was shining, but there (be) a heavy fall of snow during the night, and the snow still (lie) thick on the ground. On the previous evening, he (send) a telegram to his father, saying he would be home on Tuesday afternoon, and later that evening he (order) a taxi by telephone to take him to the station. But when he (see) the streets covered with snow, he (not think) the taxi would come.

8

I left home this morning at eight o'clock, (jump) on a bus, and (sit) down. The conductor (come) for the fare. I (put) my hand in my pocket for the money, but it (be) empty. I (forget) my money. I (leave) it on the table in my bedroom. I (have) to get off the bus and go home again. I (be) half an hour late at the office that morning. I (never be) late before.

9

When the farmer returned to the farmhouse, it was quite dark. The sun (set) an hour earlier. He (begin) work soon after sunrise. First, he (milk) the cows, and then he (plough) a big field. At lunchtime he (eat) a few sandwiches. In the afternoon he (take) some sheep to market. He (be) tired and hungry when he got home, and after supper he (fall) asleep in his chair.

10

Ali flew back to Cairo last October after he (take) a degree in English at London University. His parents (meet) him at Cairo Airport. He (not see) them for three years. They (feel) very proud of him when he (tell) them that he (pass) all his examinations with high marks. He was happy to be home again, for sometimes he (be) lonely in London, away from his family and friends.

11

Major Smith retired from the Army in the summer of 1962, when he (be) fifty years old. He (join) the Army in 1932, and during the war (fight) in North Africa and Italy. When he left the Army, he (go) to live with his elder brother, who (be) in business all his life.

12

The ship sank soon after dawn on Wednesday. There (be) a terrible storm the day before, and during the night the wind and the waves (drive) the ship on to some dangerous rocks. The captain was the last man to get into a lifeboat; he refused to leave the ship until all the passengers and crew (be) saved. When he reached the shore, he (tell) the newspaper men who were waiting to question him that he (never see) such a storm.

3 The Future Perfect tense: shall, will have + Part 3

Read the following carefully:

William Green finished his education last year, and started

work on January 1st of this year. His salary is £50 a month. He is a sensible young man, and he saves £10 a month. It is now the end of July.

How much has he saved?
He's (he has) saved £70. (7 months × £10)

The question and answer are in the Present Perfect tense, because we are speaking about NOW, the end of July.

How much had he saved at the end of April?
He'd (he had) saved £40. (4 months × £10)

The question and answer are in the Past Perfect tense, because we have gone back to the PAST, to the end of April.

How much will he have saved by the end of this year?
He'll (he will) have saved £120. (12 months × £10)

The question and answer are in the Future Perfect tense, because we are looking forward to the FUTURE, to the end of this year, and speaking of the future result of saving £10 a month. Notice the preposition *by*, which is often used with this tense to express the future time: by the year 2000, by the end of next week, by tomorrow.

Exercise 5

Read carefully each of the following passages. Then ask and answer 3 questions on each, about the present, a past, and a future time. The questions and answers on the first passage are given, with the verbs printed in capitals.

1

Charles Wilson is a criminal. He robbed a bank and shot a clerk who tried to catch him, but fortunately only wounded him slightly. The judge who tried Wilson in 1960 sent him to prison for 25 years.

1 How long HAS Wilson BEEN in prison?
This question is about the present. If it is 1966 when you answer it, the answer will be:

He'S BEEN in prison for 6 years.

2 In 1964, how long HAD Wilson BEEN in prison?
He'D BEEN in prison for 4 years.

The Perfect Tenses 19

  3 By 1980, how long WILL Wilson HAVE BEEN in prison?
  He'LL HAVE BEEN in prison for 20 years.

2

John Robinson is an author. He writes detective novels. He writes one novel a year. He wrote his first novel in ~~1958~~. *1990*

  1 How many novels ——— ?
  2009 2 In 1962, how many novels ——— ?
  3 By 1978, how many novels ——— ?

Present 2009

3

2010

Ahmad is a bank clerk. He works in the National Bank. He started work in the National Bank in ~~1962~~. *1980*

1988 1 How long ——— in the National Bank?
1986 2 In 1964, how long ——— ?
1994 3 By 1972, how long ——— ?

4

When Harold Brown got married in 1963, his father lent him £1500, to help him buy a house. Harold pays back £100 a year. *1991*

2007 1 How much ——— back?
1998 2 In 1965, how much ——— back?
2015 3 By 1973, how much ——— back?

5

Mr. Mohamed Fulan is a business man. He has business interests in the United States and he flies to New York once a year. He first flew to New York in 1958.

2008 1 How many times ——— to New York?
  2 In 1962, how many times ——— ?
  3 By ~~1978~~, how many times ——— ?
2010

6

It is now 9 p.m. and the baby is fast asleep. He went to sleep at 6 p.m. and hasn't moved since then.

  1 How long ——— asleep?
  2 At 8 p.m. how long ———?
  3 By 10 p.m. how long ———?

7

Mrs. Jones spends £1 a day on food. Today is April 20th.

  1 How much ——— this month?

2 On April 15th, how much —— ?

3 By the end of April, how much —— ?

8

Today is September 15th, and I began reading this book at the beginning of the month. It's a very long book, of 500 pages, and I've only time to read 10 pages a day.

1 How many pages —— ?

2 On September 10th, how many pages —— ?

3 By the end of September, how many pages —— ?

9

Jack's father smokes one cigarette an hour. He smoked his first cigarette today at 9 a.m. and it is now 2 p.m.

1 How many cigarettes —— today?

2 At noon, how many cigarettes —— ?

3 By 9 p.m. how many cigarettes —— ?

10

The French teacher started giving private lessons to Mary on Monday, June 1st. He gives her 3 lessons a week, on Mondays, Wednesdays, and Fridays. Today is Saturday, June 13th.

1 How many lessons —— her?

2 On Saturday, June 6th, how many lessons —— ?

3 By Saturday, June 20th, how many lessons —— ?

4 The Conditional Perfect tense: would have + Part 3

This tense, and similar verb forms, will be dealt with in Chapter 6. At present, it is enough to know that it is used in Indirect Speech when the Future Perfect tense is used in Direct Speech, for example:

William Green told me, "I WILL HAVE SAVED £120 by the end of the year."

William Green told me (that) he WOULD HAVE SAVED £120 by the end of the year.

Observation 2
Sentences from Exercise 1 of Chapter 2

Which is the correct word to put in each space:
since, for, ago, yet?

1 Henry played football at school, but he hasn't played ——— he left school in 1963.
2 She hasn't taken her little boy to a theatre ———, but she took him to a cinema ——— the first time a few days ——— .
3 She bought a coat last winter, but she hasn't bought a new dress ——— 1963.
4 He felt extremely ill when he went to hospital, but he has felt much better ——— he came out of hospital a month ——— .
5 She chose her wedding dress yesterday, but she hasn't chosen any other clothes ——— .
6 He borrowed £10 three months ———. He paid back half of it last month, but he hasn't paid back the other half ——— .

Sentences from Exercises 1, 2, and 3 of Chapter 2

Is it right or wrong to put the article *the* in the spaces?

1 She spent all ——— money in her purse.
2 It's only 11 a.m. and he has already smoked twenty cigarettes; he smoked three or four before ——— breakfast.
3 Yusef had left ——— school when his father died.
4 The police caught two of ——— escaped prisoners ——— last night, but they haven't caught ——— third yet.
5 After she had locked and bolted all the doors, she went to ——— bed.
6 It rained very heavily ——— last Monday, but it hasn't rained much since then.
7 The headmistress spoke to Mary about her work at ——— beginning of the school year.
8 He lost all his money. Then he stopped playing ——— cards.
9 Mr. Jones drank a lot of coffee when he was working in ——— Middle East.
10 We answered all ——— questions. Then we left the examination room.

Sentences from the passages in Exercise 4 of Chapter 2

Put the correct prepositions in the spaces:

1 He told everybody —— home that the doctors and nurses had looked —— him very well.

2 Ali flew back to Cairo last October after he had taken a degree —— English —— London University.

3 —— the previous evening, he had sent a telegram to his father, saying he would be home —— Tuesday afternoon, and later that evening he had ordered a taxi —— telephone to take him to the station.

4 The tourists arrived —— London Airport early —— Monday morning.

5 They felt very proud —— him when he told them that he had passed all his examinations —— high marks.

6 Major Smith retired —— the army —— the summer —— 1962, when he was fifty years old.

7 She came —— —— (2 words) the shop just before closing-time.

8 The examination finished —— noon. He had written very long answers —— three questions.

9 The young man got up early —— Tuesday morning and looked —— —— (2 words) the window —— his hotel bedroom.

10 —— lunchtime he had eaten a few sandwiches. —— the afternoon he had taken some sheep to market.

3 The Passive

1 Revision

The passive is made with any tense or form of the verb *be* and Part 3, as the following sentences show:

is + Part 3
A lot of rice IS EATEN in Asia.

was + Part 3
My watch WAS STOLEN yesterday.

will be + Part 3
Do you think the thieves WILL ever BE CAUGHT?

hasn't been + Part 3
This room HASN'T BEEN SWEPT for a fortnight.

had been + Part 3
He said the newspaper HAD BEEN THROWN away.

will have been + Part 3
By the year 2500, many actresses who are famous today WILL HAVE BEEN FORGOTTEN.

would have been + Part 3
What did you say? I said that by the year 2500, many actresses who are famous today WOULD HAVE BEEN FORGOTTEN.

must be + Part 3
This letter MUST BE ANSWERED at once.

had to be + Part 3
When he was in hospital, he HAD TO BE FED; he couldn't feed himself.

can be + Part 3
Lions and tigers CAN BE SEEN in zoos.

could be + Part 3
He spoke very clearly; he COULD BE HEARD by everyone.

may be + Part 3
You MAY BE ASKED questions on grammar in the examination.

might be + Part 3
The teacher said we MIGHT BE ASKED questions on grammar.

should be + Part 3
Naughty children SHOULD BE PUNISHED.

ought to be + Part 3
He OUGHT TO BE PUNISHED severely.

going to be + Part 3
We're GOING TO BE EXAMINED at the end of the year.

to be + Part 3
He doesn't like TO BE BEATEN when he plays chess with his brother.

2 There are *reasons* for using the passive, and we shall understand these reasons if we study the following:

(a) Henry's grandfather *was killed* in the first World War.
(b) The street lamps *are lit* soon after sunset.
(c) Thousands of American cars *were exported* last year.
(d) James Green joined the army and *was sent* overseas.

(a) Who or what killed Henry's grandfather? We do not know the exact answer to this question, and in any case we are more interested in what happened to Henry's grandfather.

(b) Who lights the street lamps? We know the answer, but it is difficult to express. We are also more interested in the fact that the lamps are lit than in the people who light them.

(c) Who exported thousands of American cars? We know. American car manufacturers exported them, but our chief interest is in the exported cars, and not in the exporters.

(d) Who sent James Green overseas? We know. The army did. But by using *was sent*, we are able to keep one subject (James Green) and to make a better sentence than: James Green joined the army and the army sent him overseas. Our chief interest is also in what happened to James Green.

The reasons for using the passive are therefore: (1) our chief interest is in the subject of the passive verb, (2) we do not know the subject of the active verb, for example *killed*, (3) it is difficult to express the subject of the active verb, for example *lights*, and (4) it helps to make a better sentence, as sentence *d* above.

Exercise 1

The following sentences contain active verbs. Our chief interest is not in the subjects of these verbs, and in some cases we do not know these subjects, or cannot express them easily. So we have put question marks. Write the sentences in the passive, taking care to keep the same tenses or verb forms. The first 3 answers are given.

1 ? built these houses about twenty-five years ago.
   These houses *were built* about twenty-five years ago.
2 ? has translated Shakespeare's plays into many languages.
   Shakespeare's plays *have been translated* into many languages.
3 ? must keep the sick child warm.
   The sick child *must be kept* warm.
4 ? made her shoes in Italy.
5 ? is going to hang the murderer next Monday.
6 ? burnt the house to the ground, and ? burnt the old man and his wife to death.
7 I don't like ? to call me a fool.
8 ? has driven this car over 50,000 miles.
9 He died on Monday, and ? buried him on Tuesday.
10 ? may steal her jewels if she doesn't lock them up.
11 ? will open the new University next October.
12 ? hasn't found the lost child yet.
13 The prisoner escaped, but ? caught him a few hours later.
14 ? ought to take away and burn that rubbish.
15 That house has been empty for years; ? should pull it down.
16 ? is going to publish his new book next year.
17 ? shouldn't spoil little children.
18 ? killed thirty people and ? injured sixty-five in that terrible railway accident.
19 ? educated her abroad.
20 The police said that ? had murdered the dead man.
21 Industries increase the wealth of a country, and ? must develop them.
22 ? has furnished the new hotel beautifully.
23 ? hid the treasure in a place which no one could find.

24 I don't know who typed this letter, but I know ? typed it on a very dirty machine.
25 She looked at a lot of dresses and ? tempted her to buy the most expensive one.
26 ? can't learn a foreign language in a few days.
27 As soon as the workmen finish the job, ? will pay them.
28 The dog was mad and ? had to shoot it.
29 The inspector told the teacher that ? might transfer him to a bigger school.
30 The Minister promised that ? wouldn't raise the price of food.

3 Only one sentence in this chapter contained a passive verb followed by the preposition *by*. This sentence was:

> He spoke very clearly; he could be heard *by* everyone.

Everyone can be called the active subject, which is used with the active verb:

> He spoke very clearly; everyone could hear him.

In most passive sentences, the active subject is NOT mentioned, but here are some examples when it is mentioned, after the preposition *by*:

(a) The little girl was run over by a bus.
(b) The sick man has just been taken to hospital by ambulance.
(c) Do you see that tree? It was struck by lightning.

These 3 sentences are in the passive for one reason: our chief interest is in the subject of the passive verb. We are interested in what happened to the little girl, to the sick man, and to the tree. We are less interested in whether a bus or a car ran over the little girl; whether an ambulance or a taxi or a private car has just taken the sick man to hospital, and what damaged or destroyed the tree.

Exercise 2

Arrange the following words into sentences, using *by*. The verbs in brackets are Part 1; you must use Part 3 in your sentences.

Example: The government ——— are (pay) ——— post office workers
Answer : Post office workers are paid by the government.

The Passive 27

1 Arabic ——— about seventy million people ——— is (speak)
2 their son ——— at the station ——— were (meet) ——— Mr. and Mrs. Brown
3 will be (teach) ——— Mr. Green ——— this class ——— next year
4 some children ——— was (find) ——— the body of the murdered man ——— playing in the forest
5 this film ——— at least a million people ——— has been (see)
6 at 2 a.m. ——— the bell ringing ——— was (wake) up ——— the doctor
7 are often (tear) ——— the woman who washes them ——— my shirts
8 for several hours ——— was (question) ——— the police ——— he
9 prefer ——— a man ——— to be (teach) ——— most boys
10 was (blow) off ——— my hat ——— the wind
11 an earthquake ——— was almost (destroy) ——— the city
12 were (break) ——— all the shop windows ——— the mob
13 her birthday ——— any of her friends ——— wasn't (forget)
14 was badly (cut) ——— the broken glass ——— his face
15 his married daughter ——— the old man ——— is (look) after
16 must be (obey) ——— everyone ——— the laws of a country
17 children ——— their grandparents ——— are often (spoil)
18 submarines ——— were (sink) ——— hundreds of ships ——— in the war
19 was (shoot) ——— the guard ——— trying to escape ——— the prisoner
20 a snake ——— have never been (bite) ——— I
21 can't be (see) ——— germs ——— the naked eye
22 a few pupils ——— was (do) correctly ——— this very difficult exercise
23 were (shake) ——— all the houses in the street ——— the explosion
24 the teacher ——— who behave badly ——— are sometimes (send) ——— pupils ——— out of class
25 this book ——— a very young author ——— was (write)

4 We learnt in Book 3 that some verbs can take two Objects, a Direct and an Indirect Object, for example:

> When an officer gives *a soldier* (Indirect Object) *an order* (Direct Object), he must obey it.
>
> No-one taught *Henry's father* (Indirect Object) *French* (Direct Object) at school.

These sentences can be expressed in the passive:

> When a soldier *is given* an order, he must obey it.
> Henry's father *wasn't taught* French at school.

Notice that the Indirect Objects become the Subjects of the passive verbs *is given* and *wasn't taught*. Notice also that it is not necessary to mention the Subjects (an officer, no-one) of the active verbs *gives* and *taught*.

Exercise 3

Express the following sentences in the passive. Do NOT mention the Subjects of the active verbs. The first two sentences are done for you.

1. The oil company has offered my brother a very good job.
   My brother *has been offered* a very good job.
2. The policeman asked me my name and address.
   I *was asked* my name and address.
3. Someone told us a very funny story yesterday.
4. Her uncle left her a lot of money.
5. The officials refused some of the travellers permission to land.
6. They have never taught that rude boy good manners.
7. The people gave the Minister a hearty welcome.
8. His employers haven't paid him his salary for last month yet.
9. The house agents showed Mr. and Mrs. Brown some very nice flats.
10. The secretary didn't tell me the exact time of my appointment.
11. The judge will give him a fair trial.
12. The teacher hasn't asked Yusef any questions in this lesson.
13. People wished the newly married couple a long and happy life.

14 They never tell me the family news.
15 His employer promised him promotion.
16 Someone has lent the shopkeeper £500.
17 The examiners didn't give us enough time to answer all the questions.
18 A guide will show the tourists most of the sights of London.
19 The rich old woman didn't leave the servants anything.
20 People sent the Minister hundreds of telegrams.
21 We should give all children the best possible education.
22 The police have promised him a reward of £50.
23 He didn't tell me the whole truth.
24 We must teach everyone how to read and write.
25 He asked her her age.

5 Read these two sentences, and notice the prepositions printed in italics:

(a) He's very sensitive, and doesn't like people to laugh *at* him.
(b) The bedroom was empty, and no-one had slept *in* the bed.

We can express these sentences in the passive:

(a) He's very sensitive, and doesn't like *to be laughed at*.
(b) The bedroom was empty, and the bed *hadn't been slept in*.

It is clearly not necessary to add to Sentence (a) 'by people'. Instead of the negative Subject (no-one) of the active verb *had slept*, we have used a negative passive verb *hadn't been slept*.

Exercise 4

Express in the passive the *second* of each of the following pairs of sentences. Do NOT mention the active Subjects.

Example : He seldom keeps a promise. No-one can rely on him.
Answer : He *can't be relied* on.

1 The child is very ill. Someone must send for the doctor.
2 This old car is in excellent condition. The owner has looked after it very well.

30 Lesson 3

3 The Prime Minister spoke for two hours. The people listened to him in complete silence.
4 She's going into hospital tomorrow. The doctors and nurses will take good care of her.
5 That little boy is very thin and always dirty. No-one looks after him properly.
6 The new servant girl is always breaking things in the kitchen. Someone should speak to her about her carelessness.
7 Shakespeare was born about 400 years ago. People look upon him as the greatest of English poets.
8 The thieves broke into the bank at midnight and stole £20,000. No-one sent for the police (plural) until eight o'clock the next morning.
9 He's a sensible man. People should listen to his advice carefully.
10 The dentist said her teeth were very bad. No-one had taken care of them.
11 Little children often ask silly questions. We shouldn't laugh at them.
12 He never broke a promise in his life. People could always rely on him.

Observation 3

Sentences taken from any of the exercises in Chapter 3

Put these 10 adjectives in the right spaces:

complete – exact – excellent – fair – hearty – lost – naked – possible – sensible – terrible

1 Germs can't be seen by the ——— eye.
2 He's a ——— man. People should listen to his advice carefully.
3 The people gave the Minister a ——— welcome.
4 Thirty people were killed and sixty-five injured in that ——— railway accident.
5 The secretary didn't tell me the ——— time of my appointment.
6 The Prime Minister spoke for two hours. The people listened to him in ——— silence.
7 The ——— child hasn't been found yet.

8 The judge will give him a ——— trial.
9 We should give all children the best ——— education.
10 This old car is in ——— condition. The owner has looked after it very well.

Is it right or wrong to put the article *a* in the spaces?

1 People wished the newly married couple ——— long and happy life.
2 The prisoner escaped, but was caught ——— few hours later.
3 The officials refused some of the travellers ——— permission to land.
4 I don't like to be called ——— fool.
5 She's going into hospital tomorrow. The doctors and nurses will take ——— good care of her.
6 This film has been seen by at least ——— million people.
7 His employer promised him ——— promotion.
8 A foreign language can't be learnt in ——— few days.

Put these 5 words in the right spaces:

away – down – off – out – up

1 My hat was blown ——— by the wind.
2 Pupils who behave badly are sometimes sent ——— of class by the teacher.
3 That rubbish ought to be taken ——— and burnt.
4 Her jewels may be stolen if she doesn't lock them ———.
5 That house has been empty for years; it should be pulled ———.

4 The Continuous Tenses

The Continuous tenses are made with any tense or form of the verb *be* and the Present Participle (-ing). The Continuous tenses are very important, for they are used today much more often than they were in the past.

1 The Present Continuous tense: am, is, are + -ing.

(a) Compare the uses of the Present Continuous tense and the simple Present tense in the following:

> We *are having* an English lesson now. We *are having* a lesson on the Continuous tenses. We *have* five or six English lessons a week.

The Continuous tense *are having* is used for something which is happening now, at the time when the sentence is said. The English lesson is taking place at this moment, it is continuing, and it is NOT finished. The simple Present tense is used for something which happens regularly, each week in the above example.

> What is Mary doing? She *is making* a summer dress. She is very clever with her needle, and always (often, sometimes) *makes* her own dresses.

The Continuous tense *is making* is used to describe what Mary is doing now, at the time when the question is asked. It also shows that the dress is NOT yet finished. The simple Present tense *makes* is used to describe a habitual action: it is Mary's habit to make always or often or sometimes her own dresses.

When we use the Continuous tense, perhaps the most important meaning which we wish to give is that some action or happening is NOT finished. The tense is therefore often used with the adverb *still*, for example:

> Has it stopped raining yet? No, it's still raining hard.

Notice the position of *still*, between *is* and *raining*.

Exercise 1

Put the verbs between brackets into the Present Continuous OR the simple Present tense. When the sentence contains the adverb *still*, be careful to put it in the correct position.

1. She usually (wear) a blue dress, but today she (wear) a grey one.
2. What's your brother doing? He (do) the crossword in the newspaper. He (do) it every day.
3. I'm afraid I'll lose this game of chess. I (play) very badly. I usually (play) much better.
4. The little boy has just fallen down and cut his knee. It still (bleed).
5. What's she doing? She (mend) her husband's socks. She always (mend) them.
6. Yes, you can borrow my dictionary. I (use) it a great deal, but I (not use) it at this moment.
7. Jack usually (sit) in the front of the class, but this morning he (sit) at the back.
8. What's the maid doing? She (make) the beds. She always (make) them as soon as breakfast is finished.
9. The bell (ring) at the beginning and end of each lesson, but it (not ring) now.
10. Ahmad (do) his homework before supper. Has he finished his homework? No, he still (do) it.
11. Where's the old man living now? He (live) with his married daughter. He usually (live) with her for six months every year.
12. The sun (set) early in the winter, but now it's June; it's 9 p.m. and the sun (set).
13. Henry usually (listen) very carefully to the teacher, but he (not listen) now; he's looking out of the window.
14. Where's your father? He's in the bathroom. He (shave). He often (shave) twice a day.
15. He's a night watchman. He works at night and (sleep) in the daytime. It's now noon, and he still (sleep).
16. Mr. Brown usually (teach) Class A, but this year he (teach) Class B.
17. He wants to buy a car, but first he must learn how to drive, so he (take) driving lessons.

18 Why is she so quiet? She (think) of her family. She's away from home, and she often (think) of them.
19 Why are you walking so quickly? I (walk) quickly because I'm cold. I never (walk) quickly in the summer.
20 It's a beautiful day and the sun (shine).
21 What are they talking about? They (talk) about politics. They always (talk) about politics when they see each other.
22 He's a very hard worker. He often (work) until midnight. It's 11 p.m. now and he still (work).
23 Is Mary ready to come out? No, she still (dress).
24 He often (read) detective novels; he (read) a very good one now.

(b) Another common use of the Present Continuous tense is seen in the following:

(*It is NOW 11 a.m.*)

What *are* you *doing* this evening?

I'm meeting Yusef at six o'clock, and *we're going* to the cinema. After the cinema, *we're having* dinner together.

The question was asked and answered at 11 a.m. so 'this evening' is in the future, the near future. The Present Continuous tense is often used when we are speaking about the near future.

Exercise 2

Put the verbs between brackets into the Present Continuous tense. Notice the near future in each case. Use the short forms, as in the above answer (I'm meeting etc.)

1 (*Today is December 10th*)
The British Prime Minister (fly) to New York on December 13th. He (take) several secretaries with him.
2 (*It is now 11 a.m*)
My uncle (arrive) this afternoon. He (come) by the 3 p.m. train. I (meet) him at the station.
3 (*Today is April 1st*)
They (get married) on April 8th. They (spend) their honeymoon in Paris.

4 (*Today is May 15th*)
   Ahmad (leave) school at the end of June, and he (start) work at the beginning of August.

5 (*Today is Monday*)
   I (go) to London on Wednesday morning, and I (stay) there until Saturday.

6 (*It is January*)
   My eldest brother (leave) his present job in the spring; he (start) a business of his own in the summer.

7 (*Today is Tuesday*)
   Can you come on Friday? It's Mary's birthday, and we (have) a party. About ten people (come).

8 (*Today is Thursday*)
   I (go) to the seaside on Sunday if it's fine. Why don't you come with me? I (take) my car.

9 (*Today is September 5th*)
   Mary's birthday is on September 15th. Her father (give) her a gold bracelet.

10 (*Today is Monday*)
   We (fly) to Beirut tomorrow and (return) to Cairo on Friday.

11 (*It is now 11.30 a.m.*)
   Have you seen John this morning? No, I (see) him this afternoon. He (come) to tea at five.

12 (*Today is March 5th*)
   The next football match is on March 8th. We (play) the new Secondary School.

2 The Future Continuous tense: shall, will be + -ing

We have seen that the Present Continuous tense is often used when we are speaking about the near, or the immediate future. The use of the Future Continuous tense is shown in the following:

> The doctor's over sixty, but he doesn't want to retire. I think he'll still be working when he's seventy.

The doctor will be seventy years old in the future, but this future is not very near, or immediate, and we therefore use the Future Continuous tense *will be working*. We use the Continuous instead of the simple Future tense *will work* because the doctor's work will NOT be finished when he is seventy.

> Mr. Fulan is going to America next month, but no-one knows how long he'll be staying there.

The Present Continuous tense *is going* is used because 'next month' is a near future. No-one knows when Mr. Fulan will leave America, except that it will be in the future. In such cases, we often prefer to use the Future Continuous tense, here *will be staying*. This tense is therefore often used when the future date is unknown, or uncertain.

Exercise 3

Put the verbs between brackets into the Future Continuous tense. The resulting sentences will be correct and natural English. Notice the uses of the Present Continuous tenses to express a near future.

1 I'm seeing Henry tomorrow, but I don't know when I (see) his brother.
2 Mr. Brown is retiring soon; he (not teach) in this school much longer.
3 The two boys are at boarding school, but they (come) home for the summer holidays.
4 Ahmad is going to the cinema this evening, but I can't go with him. I (do) my homework.
5 The old man refuses to buy a new overcoat. He's worn the same coat for ten years. I think he still (wear) it in 1980, if he's alive then.
6 It was raining hard when we went into the cinema, and I'm afraid it still (rain) when we come out.
7 She's going into hospital tomorrow; she doesn't know when she (come) out.
8 Do you think your father still (work) when he's sixty-five?
9 When the thief was sent to prison for five years, his wife said to him, "When you come out, I (wait) for you."
10 My friend's going away next week for his summer holidays, but I'm very busy. I'm afraid I (not have) a holiday this year.
11 Do you think you still (learn) English in 1975?

12 I'm going away tomorrow; I don't know for how long. You can use my car while I'm away. I (not need) it until I come back.
13 Mr. and Mrs. Smith are moving soon. They (not live) in that old house much longer.
14 Mr. Walker is spending next winter in Egypt. He (enjoy) the Egyptian sunshine while his friends are shivering in England.
15 The Pyramids are thousands of years old, but they still (stand) when we are all dead.
16 Yusef is only twenty-five, and he's earning a good salary. He probably (earn) £3000 a year when he's thirty-five.
17 I'm going to have a bathe this afternoon. It's cloudy now. I hope the sun (shine) when I get on the beach.
18 On November 1st, she wrote to her son who was abroad: "Your birthday is on November 20th. I (think) of you on that day."
19 I went to see my friend in hospital yesterday. I hope he (feel) better the next time I visit him.
20 Mahmoud is going to London next month; he (not come) home for two or three years.

Note: When the adverbs *still* or *probably* were in a sentence, did you put them in the right place, for example: he will (he'll) *still* be working; he'll *probably* be earning.

3 The Past Continuous tense: was, were + -ing

We have learnt in Book 3 that this tense is often used after the conjunctions when, while, as (just as) in sentences like the following:

(a) Ahmad wrote home once a week when he was studying in the United States.

(b) Someone rang the front door bell while Henry was having a bath.

(c) Mary dropped her purse as (just as) she was coming out of the shop.

Past Continuous tenses are used in these sentences to give the meaning of unfinished actions or happenings. Ahmad had NOT finished studying in America; Henry had NOT finished his bath; Mary had NOT finished coming out of the shop.

Compare these sentences:

  (a) When I went out this morning, it was raining hard.
  (b) When I saw her, she was wearing a blue coat.
  (c) When he came home from work, his wife was cooking the dinner.

The conjunction *when* is followed in each case by a simple Past tense, but the Continuous tenses (was raining, was wearing, was cooking) again express unfinished or continuing actions or happenings. It had NOT finished raining; she continued, of course, to wear a blue coat; his wife had NOT finished cooking.

Read these sentences:

  (a) The pupil said, "I don't understand this sentence." The teacher answered, "Of course you don't understand. You weren't listening while I was explaining it."
  (b) In 1943 (during the war), John Smith was working in a London office, while his younger brother was fighting in Italy.

Notice the two Past Continuous tenses in one sentence, in (a) *weren't listening* and *was explaining*, and in (b) *was working* and *was fighting*. In (a), the pupil continued not listening while the teacher continued and did NOT finish explaining. In (b), John Smith continued working in London while his brother continued fighting in Italy.

Past Continuous tenses are often used in narration (telling a story of any kind), for example:

> One winter evening, the old man and his wife were sitting by the fire. He was smoking his pipe and reading the paper. His wife was knitting a pair of socks. Suddenly there was a loud knock at the door. The old man got up and went out of the room.

The Past Continuous tenses *were sitting*, *was smoking*, *(was) reading*, and *was knitting* are used to describe the situation, and the simple Past tenses *was*, *got up*, and *went out* are used to describe what happened in this situation. In other words, the Past Continuous tenses are like the frame of a picture, and the simple Past tenses are used to paint the picture itself.

Exercise 4

Put the verbs between brackets into the Past Continuous OR the simple Past tense:

A

When Mr. Black left his office at 6 p.m. it (rain) hard. He (not wear) a raincoat or (carry) an umbrella, so he (run) as quickly as he could to the nearest bus-stop. As he (run), he bumped into an elderly woman and nearly (knock) her over. She was very angry and (ask) him why he didn't look where he (go). He (say) he was sorry, and (start) running again. He (get) to the bus-stop just as the bus (begin) to move, and (jump) on.

B

One fine summer afternoon, all the Smith family were in the garden. Mr. Smith (lie) on the grass under a tree. He (have) a book in his hand, but he (not read) it; he (think) about his job. His wife (pick) flowers, and their two children, a boy and a girl, (play) with a ball. After a time, the boy got tired of playing. He (throw) the ball hard at his sister, but she (not look). She (not catch) the ball, and it (break) the sitting-room window.

C

One rainy day, a fat boy (walk) along the street, eating a banana. There was an old gentleman behind him, who (held) an umbrella over his head. The boy (throw) the banana skin on the pavement. The old gentleman (step) on it, and (fall) on his back. He (drop) his umbrella and the wind (blow) it into the road. While he (lie) on the pavement, a bus (run) over his umbrella. A lady who (pass) helped the old gentleman to his feet, and the fat boy (pick) up his umbrella.

D

It was midnight, and the main street of the small town (be) empty, except for one man. He (stand) outside a shop on the corner of the street. A policeman turned the corner, and when he (see) the man, he (ask) him what he (do). The man (say) he (wait) for a friend, but the policeman (not believe) him. He (ask) him if he lived in the town. The man said no, he (stay) at a hotel for a few days. He (tell) the policeman the name of the hotel.

E

When Mr. Black came home from work, his wife (be) busy in the kitchen. She (get) the supper ready. He (ask) her what the children (do). She (say) they were both in the sitting-room; Bob (do) his homework, and Joan (watch) television. Mr. Black was tired after his day's work. He (sit) down, and while his wife (lay) the table, he (tell) her what he had done in the office.

4 The Perfect Continuous tenses:

(a) **Present:** have, has been + -ing
(b) **Past:** had been + -ing
(c) **Future:** shall, will have been + -ing

Read the following:

Ahmad began learning English in 1960. It is now 1965, and he's still learning English. He hasn't finished learning English yet. He'll probably continue learning English for two or three more years.

We can now make 3 sentences, using Perfect Continuous tenses:

(a) Ahmad's (Ahmad has) been learning English since 1960 *or* for five years (1960–1965).

We use the Continuous tense *has been learning* because Ahmad has NOT finished and will probably continue learning.

(b) In 1962, Ahmad had been learning English for two years.

The Past Perfect Continuous tense *had been learning* is used because we have gone back to a past year, 1962.

(c) By 1968, Ahmad will have been learning English for eight years.

The Future Perfect Continuous tense *will have been learning* is used because we have gone forward to a future year, 1968.

Here is another example of the use of these three Continuous tenses:

> The Prime Minister began his speech at 7 p.m. It is now 8.30 p.m. and he's still speaking. He'll probably continue speaking.
>
> (a) The Prime Minister has been speaking since 7 p.m. *or* for an hour and a half (7 – 8.30 p.m.)
> (b) At 8 p.m. he had been speaking for an hour.
> (c) By 9 p.m. he'll have been speaking for two hours.

In sentence (a), we are speaking about the present time (8.30 p.m.). In sentence (b), we have gone back to a past time (8 p.m.). In sentence (c), we have gone forward to a future time (9. p.m.)

In both these examples, about Ahmad learning English, and about the Prime Minister's speech, we used Continuous and not simple tenses because we were describing activities which were continuing, and would probably continue in the future.

Exercise 5 (On the Present Perfect Continuous tense)

A Answer the following questions in complete sentences:

1 How long have you been learning English?
2 How long have I been teaching you English?
3 How long have you been living in this city (town, village)?
4 Have you got a younger brother (sister) who goes to school? How long has he (she) been going to school?
5 Have you got a brother who goes to work? Where is he working? How long has he been working there?

B Read the following carefully, and then write sentences using the Present Perfect Continuous tense. In each sentence use *since* AND *for*, as in this example:

> He began reading the newspaper at three o'clock. It's now five o'clock, and he's still reading the newspaper.

Answer: He's been reading the newspaper *since* three o'clock, or *for* two hours.

1 I began listening to the wireless at six o'clock. It's now seven o'clock, and I'm still listening to the wireless.
2 It began raining on Monday. It's now Wednesday, and it's still raining.

3 She began washing clothes at nine o'clock. It's now twelve o'clock, and she's still washing clothes.

4 We began watching television at seven o'clock. It's now eight o'clock, and we're still watching television.

5 The little girl began to feel unwell on Tuesday. It's now Friday, and she's still feeling unwell.

6 I began waiting for a bus at eight o'clock. It's now twenty past eight, and I'm still waiting for a bus.

7 Yusef began working in a bank in 1960. It's now 1965, and he's still working in a bank.

8 The sun began shining at six o'clock. It's now eleven o'clock, and the sun is still shining.

9 She went into the garden and sat down at four o'clock. It's now six o'clock, and she's still sitting in the garden.

10 The bell began ringing at eight o'clock. It's now five past eight, and the bell is still ringing.

11 I began writing letters at seven o'clock. It's now ten o'clock, and I'm still writing letters.

12 The water began to boil at five o'clock. It's now five past five, and the water is still boiling.

13 The little boy began going to school in January. It's now June, and the little boy is still going to school.

14 The dog began barking at nine o'clock. It's now half past nine, and the dog is still barking.

15 Ahmad went to live in Cairo in 1962. It's now 1965, and he's still living in Cairo.

16 The lorry-driver began driving at six o'clock this morning. It's now two o'clock in the afternoon, and he's still driving.

17 The four men began playing cards at eight o'clock this evening. It's now midnight, and they're still playing.

18 He put on a clean shirt on Monday morning. It's now Thursday morning, and he's still wearing this shirt.

19 Jack's grandfather began smoking in 1920, when he was twenty years old. He's now sixty-six, and he's still smoking.

20 He lost his job in May, and began looking for another job. It's now August, and he's still looking for a job.

The Continuous Tenses

Exercise 6 (On the 3 Perfect Continuous tenses)

Read the following carefully, and then write sentences using the *three* Perfect Continuous tenses, (a) about the present time, (b) about a past time, and (c) about a future time. The times are given, as in this example:

> Fatma went to live with her uncle in 1960, and she's still living with him. (Present – 1966, Past – 1962, Future – 1970)

Answer: (a) She's been living with her uncle for six years.
(b) In 1962, she'd been living with her uncle for two years.
(c) By 1970, she'll have been living with her uncle for ten years.

Note: Use the preposition *for* in each of the 3 sentences, and the preposition *by* for the future time in (c).

1. I began waiting for the doctor at ten o'clock, and I'm still waiting. (Present – eleven o'clock, Past – half past ten, Future – twelve o'clock)
2. Mahmoud began learning English in 1964, and he's still learning English. (Present – 1966, Past – 1965, Future – 1970)
3. Mr. Green began teaching in 1945, and he's still teaching. (Present – 1965, Past – 1955, Future – 1975)
4. The author bought a typewriter and began using it in 1960. He's still using this typewriter. (Present–1966, Past–1963, Future–1970)
5. She began knitting at six o'clock, and she's still knitting. (Present – seven o'clock, Past – half past six, Future – eight o'clock)
6. The old man began working in 1926, and he's still working. (Present – 1966, Past – 1956, Future – 1976)
7. There was a very long queue outside the cinema. We began standing in the queue at five o'clock, and we're still standing in the queue. (Present – half past five, Past – a quarter past five, Future – six o'clock)
8. He went to hospital on January 1st. He had to lie on his back. He's still lying on his back. (Present – April 1st, Past – March 1st, Future – June 1st)
9. I began driving at seven o'clock this morning, and I'm still driving. (Present – ten o'clock, Past – nine o'clock, Future – eleven o'clock)

10 She bought a very good pair of shoes in 1964, and she's still wearing these shoes. (Present – 1966, Past – 1965, Future – 1970)

5 Continuous tenses (passive)

There are only two Continuous tenses which are used in the passive form:

1 Present: am, is, are being + Part 3

(a) The little girl has been very ill, and the doctor says she mustn't go to school, so she *is being taught* at home.
(b) The new University *is being opened* next October.

Notice the formation: *taught* is Part 3 of the verb teach-taught-taught, and *opened* is Part 3 of the regular verb open-opened-opened. Notice also that in Sentence (a), we are speaking about the present time, but in Sentence (b) about the future, probably a near future.

2 Past: was, were being + Part 3

(a) I couldn't use my car last week; it *was being repaired*.
(b) The workmen complained that they *weren't being paid* enough.

Notice again the formation: *repaired* is Part 3 of the verb repair-repaired-repaired, and *paid* is Part 3 of the verb pay-paid-paid.

Exercise 7

A Put the verbs between brackets into the passive form of the Present Continuous tense. After each sentence, answer this question: Are we speaking about the present time, or about a near future?

1 I'm not wearing my black shoes today. They (mend).
2 The old gentleman died a month ago; his house and furniture (sell) next week.
3 Thousands of new houses (build) every year.
4 The secretary said, "The letters will be ready in a few minutes. They (type) now."
5 The murderer (hang) tomorrow morning.
6 He hopes to have his new suit soon. It (make) by a first-class tailor.

The Continuous Tenses

7 The children are very excited this morning. They (take) to the circus this afternoon.
8 You can't go into the sitting-room. The walls (paint).
9 He was taken to hospital this afternoon, and (operate on) tomorrow morning.
10 The little girl is an only child, and she (spoil) by her parents and grandparents.

B Put the verbs between brackets into the passive form of the Present OR Past Continuous tense.

1 When I saw the car, it (drive) at over fifty miles an hour.
2 The author's new book (publish) next month.
3 When the doctor called to see the baby, it (feed).
4 Mr. Brown is leaving this school in a month's time. He (transfer) to another school.
5 She told her new employer, "I left my last job because I (not pay) enough."
6 The parcel should arrive very soon; it (send) by air.
7 The pickpocket didn't know that he (watch) by a policeman in plain clothes (not in uniform).
8 It was very cold yesterday afternoon, but we couldn't light a fire in the sitting-room; the chimney (sweep).
9 The little boy's mother is in hospital; he (look after) by his aunt.
10 I think Ahmad will pass the examination; he (give) extra lessons.
11 The Minister of Education (ask) to open the new University next month.
12 He told me that the cupboards (make) by a local carpenter.
13 The old woman died yesterday, and she (bury) tomorrow.
14 Her parents are in India, but she (educated) in England.
15 It was a lonely road, and the girl was afraid; she thought she (follow).

Observation 4
Sentences from Exercises 1 and 3 only of Chapter 4

There is an adverb between brackets at the end of each of the following sentences. Put this adverb in a correct position in the sentence.

1 It was raining hard when we went into the cinema, and I'm afraid it will be raining when we come out. (still)
2 Jack sits in the front of the class. (usually)
3 I walk quickly in the summer. (never)
4 He'll be earning £3000 a year when he's thirty-five. (probably)
5 The little boy has fallen down and cut his knee. (just)
6 He works until midnight. (often)
7 Do you think you'll be learning English in 1975? (still)
8 He shaves twice a day. (often)
9 They talk about politics when they see each other. (always)
10 Has he finished his homework? No, he's doing it. (still)

Sentences from Exercises 2, 5, 6, and 7 of Chapter 4

Which is the correct preposition to put in each space, *at*, *in*, or *on*?

1 He went to hospital ——— January 1st.
2 Ahmad went to live in Cairo ——— 1962.
3 Mr. Brown is leaving this school ——— a month's time.
4 I'm going to London ——— Wednesday morning, and I'm staying there until Saturday.
5 We began watching television ——— seven o'clock.
6 Ahmad is leaving school ——— the end of June, and he's starting work ——— the beginning of August.
7 He lost his job ——— May, and began looking for another job.
8 They're getting married ——— April 8th.
9 I'm seeing him this afternoon. He's coming to tea ——— five.
10 Jack's grandfather began smoking ——— 1920, when he was twenty years old.
11 Mary's birthday is ——— September 15th.
12 The secretary said, "The letters will be ready ——— a few minutes. They're being typed now."
13 He put on a clean shirt ——— Monday morning.
14 My eldest brother is leaving his present job ——— the spring; he's starting a business of his own ——— the summer.

5 One Future Tense Only

1 The conjunctions *if* and *unless* are followed by a Present tense in sentences about the future, for example:
   (a) If you *don't go* to bed early tonight, you'll feel very tired tomorrow morning.
   (b) You won't catch the first train tomorrow unless you *get up* at 5 a.m.

In Sentence (a) 'tonight', and in Sentence (b) '5 a.m.' are *future* times, but Present tenses 'don't go' and 'get up' are used. In such sentences, ONE Future tense is enough.

The Present tense, referring to a future time, may be Continuous:

   (a) I've got a bad headache. I won't come to school tomorrow unless *I'm feeling* better.
   (b) I'll come with you tomorrow if *you're going* to the shops.

2 Now read these sentences:
   (a) She'll be twenty-five *before* she *finishes* her education.
   (b) I'll pay this bill at the end of the month, *when* I *get* my salary.

After the conjunctions *before* and *when*, Present tenses (*finishes* and *get*) are used, although they refer to a future time. In such sentences, ONE Future tense is enough.

   (a) Mary said to her sister, "I'll come for a walk with you *when I've finished* my homework."
   (b) He's very foolish. He'll go on gambling *until* he *has lost* all his money.

In these two sentences, the conjunctions *when* and *until* are followed by Present Perfect tenses, which, as we have said before, are really present tenses.

We can now make an important general rule:

   In English, only ONE Future tense is necessary in sentences about the future which contain certain conjunctions. After these conjunctions, a Present tense (simple or Continuous) or a Present

Perfect tense is used. These conjunctions are: if, unless, and 'time' words such as before, when, until, as soon as, after.

Exercises

1 Put the verbs between brackets into the *simple* Present or Future tense:

1 I'm afraid the old woman (die) before she (see) her son.
2 The teacher said, "I (begin) the lesson as soon as Jack (stop) talking."
3 The old gentleman doesn't go out in the winter. He (go) out when the weather (get) warmer.
4 I (wait) for the doctor until he (come) back from the hospital.
5 Ahmad (not pass) the examination next summer unless he (work) much harder.
6 He (have) a bad accident if he (not drive) more carefully.
7 She's flying to Cairo tomorrow. She (send) her family a telegram as soon as she (arrive).
8 She told her guests, "We (have) lunch when my son (come) home from school."
9 The teacher said, "I (not retire) before I (be) sixty-five."
10 You (be) late unless you (take) a taxi.
11 I (not speak) to him again unless he (apologise).
12 His father (not lend) him any more money until he (learn) not to waste it.
13 We (have) a picnic tomorrow if it (be) a fine day.
14 I (finish) reading this book before I (go) to bed.
15 Mr. Smith is retiring next year. He (have) nothing to do when he (retire).
16 She (mend) his socks if he (ask) her to.
17 I'm sure he (write) to me as soon as he (know) my new address.
18 She's always busy in the house, and never has a rest. She (go on) working until she (drop).
19 Yusef has borrowed my dictionary. He (give) it back when he (see) me tomorrow.
20 The poor fellow's out of work, but he (pay) his debts as soon as he (find) a job.

21 The teacher (not let) Mary go home early unless she (have) a good excuse.
22 The postman (start) work tomorrow before the sun (rise).
23 The little boy (not be) happy until his father (buy) him a bicycle.
24 She (wash) my shirts tomorrow if she (have) time.
25 We (go) out when it (stop) raining.

2 Put the verbs between brackets into the Present Continuous or Future tense:

1 If you (go) abroad next week, I (not see) you again, so I'll say goodbye now.
2 She said to her husband, "I (cook) the breakfast while you (shave)."
3 The teacher told the class, "While you (answer) the questions, I (write) six more questions on the blackboard."
4 She said to her married sister, "I (look after) the baby while you (dress)."
5 I (come) with you if you (take) your car. If not, I (go) by bus.
6 He said to his secretary, "I (make) a few phone calls while you (type) these letters."
7 I (come) and see you at six o'clock this evening unless I still (work).
8 The teacher said, "This is a difficult question. I hope you (listen) very carefully while I (explain) it."
9 Ahmad is living in Beirut now. If you (go) there, you (see) him.
10 He told his friend, "Certainly I (lend) you my car tomorrow if I (not use) it myself."
11 I told him on the phone, "I (meet) you at the station tomorrow afternoon if you (come) by train."
12 I (not go) out this afternoon if it (still rain).
13 Mrs. Brown said, "I (get) the supper ready while the children (do) their homework."
14 You (need) to take warm clothes with you if you (go) to Russia in the winter.
15 I haven't time to read the paper now. I (read) it while I (have) lunch.

3 Put the verbs between brackets into the Present Perfect or Future tense:

1. He (buy) a house as soon as he (save) enough money.
2. The little boy (not stop) playing with his toy car until he (break) it.
3. Mary said, "I (go) for a walk when I (finish) my homework."
4. The doctor said, "You (feel) better after you (take) this medicine."
5. The police (go on) looking for the bank robbers until they (find) them.
6. I (not have) dinner before I (listen) to the news.
7. He (buy) a new car as soon as he (sell) his old one.
8. She told her little girl, "I (not give) you any chocolate until you (drink) all your milk."
9. The teacher told Yusef, "I'm sure you (pass) the examination if you (read) the set books carefully."
10. The merchant (not send) us the goods before we (pay) for them.
11. The manager said, "I (answer) these letters after I (have) lunch."
12. I (tell) you again if you (forget) what I told you yesterday.
13. The maid said, "I (make) the beds as soon as I (sweep) the kitchen."
14. We (invite) all our friends when we (finish) furnishing our new house.
15. I (go) to bed as soon as I (do) this job.
16. Are you going to drive all the way yourself? You (feel) very tired after you (drive) 300 miles.
17. I (tell) you if you (make) a mistake.
18. Mr. Smith said, "Where's my umbrella? I (be) angry if my son (take) it again."
19. He kissed his children goodnight and said, "I (not be) back before you (go) to bed."
20. Jack promised his teacher, "I (not leave) the examination room until I (answer) all the questions."
21. I'm very tired. I (start) work again when I (have) a rest.

22 I'm seeing the doctor this evening. I (tell) you what he says after I (see) him.
23 Jack's father was angry with him, but he said, "I (not punish) you before I (hear) your story."
24 I know very little about the present Prime Minister. I (know) more when I (read) his biography.

4 The Future tense may be Continuous (shall, will be + -ing)

Put the verbs between brackets into the Future Continuous or Present tense:

1 Ahmad's only twenty-one, but he's very good at his work. He (earn) a high salary when he (be) thirty.
2 Mary's mother (wait) for her when she (come) out of school.
3 It was raining hard when we went into the cinema. I hope it (not rain) when we (come) out.
4 When Jack went to India, his mother told him, "I (think) of you every day while you (be) away."
5 How long is he staying at that hotel? He (stay) there until his brother (arrive).
6 She still (do) the housework if her husband (come) home before four o'clock.
7 The doctor said, "I hope you (feel) better when I next (see) you."
8 Mr. Thomas has applied for a job as an English teacher in Indonesia. This time next year he (teach) English in Indonesia if he (get) the job.
9 I told the electrician not to come before 2 p.m. If he (come) before then, we still (have) lunch.
10 I'm going away tomorrow for a holiday at the seaside. At this time tomorrow I (bathe) if the water (be) warm enough.
11 The lorry-driver has a long journey tomorrow. He (drive) all day unless his lorry (break) down.
12 He told his secretary, "You can go home now. I'm expecting a phone call from Mr. Williams. I (not leave) the office until he (phone)."
13 Mary said, "I still (do) my homework when my father (come) home from the office."

14 Do you think you still (live) here when you (be) forty?

15 I expect I (watch) television all this evening unless someone (call) on me.

Note: When the adverb *still* occurred in the above sentences, did you put it in the right position: shall, will *still* be ——?

Observation 5

Sentences from the four exercises in Chapter 5

Choose the right joining word (conjunction) to put in each space from these 5:

after – as soon as – before – until – while

1 The police will go on looking for the bank robbers —— they have found them.

2 I haven't time to read the paper now. I'll read it —— I'm having lunch.

3 I'll finish reading this book —— I go to bed.

4 Are you going to drive all the way yourself? You'll feel very tired —— you've driven 300 miles.

5 When Jack went to India, his mother told him, "I'll be thinking of you every day —— you're away."

6 She's flying to Cairo tomorrow. She'll send her family a telegram —— she arrives.

7 I'm afraid the old woman will die —— she sees her son.

8 How long is he staying at that hotel? He'll be staying there —— his brother arrives.

9 The doctor said, "You'll feel better —— you've taken this medicine."

10 I'm sure he'll write to me —— he knows my new address.

11 She said to her married sister, "I'll look after the baby —— you're dressing."

12 She's always busy in the house, and never has a rest. She'll go on working —— she drops.

Which is the correct verb to use, *do, have,* or *make*?

1 The maid said, "I'll (do, make) the beds as soon as I've swept the kitchen."

One Future Tense Only

2 He'll (do, have, make) a bad accident if he doesn't drive more carefully.
3 He said to his secretary, "I'll (do, make) a few phone calls while you're typing these letters."
4 Mr. Smith is retiring next year. He'll have nothing to (do, make) when he retires.
5 We'll (do, have, make) a picnic tomorrow if it's a fine day.
6 She'll still be (doing, making) the housework if her husband comes home before four o'clock.
7 I'll tell you if you've (done, made) a mistake.
8 I'm very tired. I'll start work again when I've (had, done, made) a rest.
9 I'll go to bed as soon as I've (done, made) this job.

6 Conditional Tenses

1. Study these sentences:
    - (a) Mr. Jones said, "If I *had* a big garden, I *would grow* a lot of flowers."
    - (b) He said later, "I *wouldn't like* to have a very big garden unless I *had* a gardener to help me."

would grow and *wouldn't like* are Conditional tenses. The formation is: would (not) + Part 1.

had is Part 2 of the verb *have*, but in these sentences it is NOT a Past tense, for it does NOT refer to past time. We know that Mr. Jones, at the time when he is speaking, does NOT have a big garden, and that he does NOT have a gardener.

Mr. Jones can say the first sentence in 3 ways:

  - (a) If I *had* a big garden, I *would grow* a lot of flowers.
  - (b) If I *had* a big garden, I *might grow* a lot of flowers.
  - (c) If I *had* a big garden, I *could grow* a lot of flowers.

There is a difference in meaning:

  - (a) would grow – it is *certain* that I would grow
  - (b) might grow – *perhaps* I would grow
  - (c) could grow – it would be *possible* for me to grow

These sentences in Indirect Speech are:

  - (a) Mr. Jones said that if he *had* a big garden, he *would* (*might, could*) *grow* a lot of flowers.
  - (b) He said later that he *wouldn't like* to have a very big garden unless he *had* a gardener to help him.

Notice that the verbs in Direct and Indirect Speech are the same. Mr. Jones would probably use short forms in speech and say:

   If *I'd* a big garden, *I'd* grow a lot of flowers.

Notice that the short forms of *I had* and *I would* are the same: *I'd*.

Conditional Tenses 55

Exercise 1

Use Part 2 or the Conditional tense of the verbs in brackets. Practise using the short forms *I'd, he'd* etc. for *I, he would* etc. OR *I, he had* etc.

Example 1 : If I (see) a blind man trying to cross the road, I (help) him.

Answer : If I *saw* a blind man trying to cross the road, *I'd* (*I would*) help him.

Example 2 : He (not walk) to school if he (have) a bicycle.

Answer : He *wouldn't walk* to school if *he'd* (*he had*) a bicycle.

1. If I (know) the answer, I (tell) you.
2. The journey takes about three hours by bus. You (get) there much sooner if you (go) by train.
3. The teacher told Mary that she (not pass) the examination unless she (work) harder.
4. If I (find) a lady's handbag in the street, I (take) it to the police station.
5. I (not buy) a secondhand car unless I (be) sure the engine was in good condition.
6. If we never (have) a holiday, we (soon get) tired of school.
7. I (never eat) fish unless I (know) it was fresh.
8. The teacher said to David, "You're late again this morning. If you (get up) earlier, you (not be) late so often."
9. He was a good honest man. He (never make) a promise unless he (mean) to keep it.
10. I (never drive) a car unless it (be) insured.

In the next 5 sentences, use *might* instead of *would* (to give the meaning 'perhaps'):

11. He's getting fat. If he (take) more exercise, he (lose) weight.
12. He smokes about fifty cigarettes a day and he's always coughing. If he (not smoke) so heavily, he (get) rid of his cough.
13. She feels very tired in the morning. If she (go) to bed earlier, she (not feel) so tired.
14. He's not a strong child. If he (drink) more milk, he (be) stronger.
15. Jack said, "If I (listen) to the teacher more carefully, I (make) fewer mistakes in dictation."

Lesson 6

In the next 5 sentences, use *could* instead of *would* (to give the meaning 'possible'):

16 We (understand) the English teacher better if he (speak) more slowly.
17 I like reading, but I haven't much time. If I (have) more time, I (read) a lot more.
18 I don't know where he's living now. If I (know) his address, I (write) to him.
19 If Jack's father (give) him £20, he (buy) a new bicycle.
20 James is rather short. If he (be) taller, he (wear) his brother's clothes.

Answer the following questions in complete sentences. In your answers, use the verbs in the questions: *would, might*, or *could*.

1 What would you buy if your father gave you £20?
2 Who might you see if you visited Hollywood?
3 How much would it cost if you took a taxi to school?
4 Would you be angry if someone called you a fool?
5 In which town or city would you live if you had the choice?
6 If I lent you £5, when could you pay me back?
7 Who would you ask if you didn't know the way to the post office?
8 Could you come to school an hour earlier tomorrow if the teacher asked you?
9 If a man saved £10 a month, how much would he have after a year?
10 Could you buy a good car if you had £150?
11 How would you feel if you never had a holiday?
12 Who might you sometimes see driving from the palace if you lived in London?
13 Could you wake up at 5 a.m. if no one called you?
14 How much would you earn if you became a teacher?
15 What would you do if your house caught fire?
16 Could you cook your own dinner if your mother was ill?
17 Would you stay in bed if you had a cold?
18 Could you understand an Englishman if he spoke very quickly?

19 If you had a lot of money, where would you put it?
20 If an old man fell down in the street, what might he easily break?

Note : In all the sentences in this lesson, the conjunctions *if* and *unless* were followed by Part 2 of the verb, which did not refer to past time, although it had the same form as the Past tense. In the following sentence, the form is different:

> If I *were* you, I'd take an umbrella. I think it's going to rain.

The form *were* in 'If I were ———' is still in common use, but the form *was* can also be used in sentences like these:

> If I was (or were) your father, I wouldn't let you smoke.
> If I was (or were) a millionaire, I'd probably have more than one car.

2 Study these sentences:

> When George Brown left school in 1955, he was offered a job in a bank, but he didn't take it. If he *had taken* the job, he *would* (or *might*) *be* a bank manager now.

George Brown did not take the job in 1955, in the past. We suppose the opposite, and express this with the Past Perfect tense *had taken*. The *present* result is expressed by the Conditional tense *would be* (certain) or *might be* (perhaps).

> The teacher told Ahmad, "If you *had done* your homework last night, you *could answer* my questions this morning."

Ahmad did not do his homework last night, in the past. The teacher supposes the opposite, using the Past Perfect tense *had done*. He uses *could answer* to express the present possible result.

The pattern of such sentences is:

   if, unless + Past Perfect tense / would, might, could + Part 1.

Exercise 2

Use the Past Perfect or the Conditional tense of the verbs in brackets. Practise using the short forms.

1. He retired in 1960. If he (go) on working until 1965, he (have) a bigger pension now.
2. She told the maid, "This room isn't clean. If you (sweep) it properly, there (not be) so much dust on the floor."
3. After the little boy had eaten a whole box of chocolates, his father said, "If I (eat) so many chocolates, I (feel) sick."
4. The thief was released from prison yesterday. If he (not behave) well in prison, he (still be) there.
5. The old man hasn't got enough money to live on. If he (save) more when he was young, he (not be) in need of help now.
6. He promised to pay yesterday, and he did so. If he (not pay), I (be) very angry.
7. The young man ran all the way to the office, but he wasn't out of breath. The manager said, "If I (run) so far, I (be) out of breath."
8. I had a sandwich for lunch. If I (have) a proper lunch, I (not feel) so hungry now.
9. He told his employer, "I'm not feeling very well. I (not be) here today if I (not promise) to come."
10. I can hardly keep my eyes open. If I (go) to bed earlier last night, I (not be) so tired now.

In the next 5 sentences, use *might* instead of *would* (to give the meaning 'perhaps'):

11. He wasted his time at the university. If he (study) harder, he (have) a better job today.
12. She refused to see a doctor until it was too late, and she died a month ago. If she (go) to a doctor earlier, she (be) alive today.
13. If my secretary (take) more care, she (not make) so many mistakes in typing.
14. He wasn't a very happy man, and he often said, "If I (follow) my father's advice, I (be) much happier now."
15. He looked at his watch while he was driving and thought, "If I (not stop) to get petrol, I (be) home now."

In the next 5 sentences, use *could* instead of *would* (to give the meaning 'possible'):

16. House prices are high. If you (buy) a house in 1945 for £3000, you (sell) it today for probably £6000.

17 Mr. Jones told his wife, "We (have) a car if we (not spend) so much on new furniture."
18 If Jack (not hurt) his ankle yesterday, he (play) football this afternoon.
19 She sat down after lunch and said to herself, "I (not have) a rest if I (not finish) all the housework."
20 The young man is short of money. He (not pay) his children's school fees if his father (not lend) him £50.

3 Read the following:

    I wanted to catch the nine o'clock train yesterday. I thought I had plenty of time, so I took a bus to the station. But there was a lot of traffic, and the bus kept stopping. I didn't get to the station until ten past nine, and I had to wait until eleven o'clock for the next train.

    If I *had taken* a taxi to the station,
    I *would have caught* the nine o'clock train (certain)
    I *might have caught* the nine o'clock train (perhaps)
    I *could have caught* the nine o'clock train (possible).

I did not take a taxi yesterday, in the past. I suppose the opposite, and express this by using the Past Perfect tense *had taken*. I did not catch the nine o'clock train, but I express the *past* result, if I had taken a taxi, by using the verbs *would, might, could have caught*.

would have caught is the Perfect Conditional tense. *caught* is Part 3 of the verb catch-caught-caught. The formation of this tense, and when we use *might* or *could*, is:

    would, might, could have + Part 3

Exercise 3

Use the Past Perfect or the Perfect Conditional tense of the verbs in brackets. Answer the questions which follow some of the sentences.

Example: Mary (be) late for school yesterday unless she (run) all the way.
         Was Mary late for school yesterday? Did she run all the way?
Answer : Mary *would have been* late for school yesterday unless *she'd (she had) run* all the way.
         No, she wasn't late. Yes, she ran all the way.

Lesson 6

Use *would* in these sentences:

1 I (not believe) the news unless I (hear) it on the wireless.
   Did I believe the news? Did I hear it on the wireless?
2 If I (see) you in the street yesterday, of course I (say) Good Morning.
3 If the taxi-driver (drive) more carefully, there (not be) an accident.
   Did the taxi-driver drive carefully? Was there an accident?
4 After the teacher had punished Ahmad, he told him, "I (not punish) you if you (tell) me the truth."
5 I'm sorry I threw the newspaper away. I (not throw) it away if I (know) you had wanted it.
6 Why didn't you ask me to help you? Of course I (help) you if you (ask) me to.
7 Jack's mother told him, "I (wash) your shirts yesterday if I (have) time."
   Did she wash his shirts yesterday? Did she have time?
8 I'm sorry I couldn't come to the cinema with you last Friday. I (come) if I (not be) so busy.
9 The thieves ran out of the bank, jumped into a car, and drove away. The police (never find) them if a bank clerk (not take) the number of the car.
   Did the police find the thieves? Did a bank clerk take the number of the car?
10 The clerk told his employer, "I (not leave) the office early yesterday unless I (finish) my work."

Use *might* in these sentences:

11 She (catch) a cold if she (not wear) a coat.
12 The travellers in the desert were lost. They (die) of thirst if they (not meet) some Arabs.
   Did the travellers die of thirst? Did they meet some Arabs?
13 Henry took an examination last June, but he failed. If he (answer) the last question more correctly, he (pass).
14 The little boy climbed up a tree. He (break) a leg or an arm if he (fall).
15 If you (send) the parcel by air, it (arrive) a week sooner than it did.

Conditional Tenses

Use *could* in these sentences:

16. If Henry's father (have) enough money in 1950, he (buy) a bigger house.

    Did he have enough money in 1950? Did he buy a bigger house?
17. We (send) them a Christmas card if we (know) their address.
18. The police officer told the lady, "If you (keep) all that money in the bank, no-one (steal) it."
19. If I (knew) you were coming by the 6 p.m. train, I (meet) you at the station.
20. I think we (win) the football match if we (play) a little better in the second half.

Answer the following questions in complete sentences:

1. If you had been born in 1940, how old would you have been in 1955?
2. Ahmad went to the cinema yesterday. Could you have gone with him if he had asked you?
3. If you had been late for this lesson, would you have apologised to the teacher?
4. What would you have done if there had been a holiday yesterday?
5. If you had had a slight headache yesterday, would you have come to school?
6. Could you have lent me a pound yesterday if I had needed it?
7. If you had made two mistakes in dictation last week, how many marks would you have lost?
8. His family were very poor, but he went to a university. Could he have gone to a university if he hadn't won a scholarship?
9. Would you have been late this morning if you had woken up at half past eight?
10. Could you have answered these questions if you had been absent for the last fortnight?

4 The sentences in Section 3 followed this pattern:

if, unless + Past Perfect tense / would, could, might have + Part 3

The Past Perfect Continuous tense is sometimes used after *if* or *unless*, for example:

> It was raining quite hard, but Mary went out wearing thin sandals, and her feet soon got wet. If she *had been wearing* thick shoes, she *wouldn't have got* her feet wet.

The Continuous tense is used to express that the wearing of thin sandals continued and was not finished when Mary got her feet wet.

Exercise 4

Use the Past Perfect Continuous or the Perfect Conditional tense of the verbs in brackets.

Use *would* in these sentences:

1 Mrs. Smith isn't a very good driver and she had an accident a week ago. There (not be) an accident if her husband (drive).

2 The teacher told Jack, "You (understand) me if you (listen) instead of looking out of the window."

3 The little boy (not fall) into the river if his mother (look after) him properly.

4 An old man was knocked down by a bus while I was looking in a shop window. I (see) the accident if I (not look) in a shop window.

5 The captain (not give) the order to leave the ship if it (not sink).

6 Jack answered the phone. His father (answer) the phone if he (not have) a bath.

Use *might* in these sentences:

7 When she opened the door, the kitchen was full of gas. If she (smoke), there (be) an explosion.

8 I don't watch television very often. I (do) so last night if I (not read) a very interesting book.

9 We lost the football match yesterday, but we (win) if our best player (play).

Use *could* in these sentences:

10 I sat at the back of the theatre and couldn't hear very well. If I (sit) nearer the stage, I (hear) better.

11 Mr. Brown couldn't buy a car in 1955, because his salary was too small. He (buy) a car if he (earn) a better salary.
12 I was too busy last night to come and have dinner with you. I (come) if I (not work).
13 If you (learn) English fifty years ago, you (not listen) to English by Radio.
14 Fortunately it stopped snowing some hours ago. We (not take) the car if it still (snow).
15 He felt better yesterday and (go) for a walk if it (not rain) hard.

5 Study the following:

> When George Brown left school in 1955, he was offered a job in a bank, but he didn't take it. If his brother *had been offered* that job, he *would have taken* it.

had been offered is the passive form of the Past Perfect tense.

> I'm expecting a letter from Paris. I think I would have got it yesterday if it *had been sent* by air.

had been sent is the passive form of the Past Perfect tense. The passive formation of this tense is:

> had been + Part 3 (offered, sent)

> There was a very bad accident, but fortunately he was sitting at the back of the car. If he had been sitting next to the driver, he *would have been killed*.

would have been killed is the passive form of the Perfect Conditional tense, *might* or *could* can also be used, for example:

> We won the football match, but we *might have been beaten* if we hadn't scored a lucky goal.
> The work *could have been finished* yesterday if there hadn't been a holiday.

The passive formation of the Perfect Conditional tense is:

> would, might, could have been + Part 3 (killed, beaten, finished)

Exercise 5

A Use the passive form of the Past Perfect tense of the verbs in brackets. Answer the questions which follow some of the sentences, for example:

> The typist wouldn't have left the office early unless she (give) permission. Did she leave the office early? Was she given permission?
>
> The typist wouldn't have left the office early unless she *had been given* permission. Yes, she did (leave the office early). Yes, she was (given permission).

1 This suit is ready-made. It would have cost more if it (make) to measure.

2 The sick man might have died if he (not take) to hospital immediately. Did the sick man die? Was he taken to hospital immediately?

3 Mr. and Mrs. Jones never went out in the evening; their little girl would have been afraid if she (leave) alone in the house.

4 The teacher would have corrected Mary's composition if it (write) in ink and not in pencil. Did the teacher correct Mary's composition? Was her composition written in ink?

5 When Ahmad returned from London to Kuwait, he would have been disappointed if he (not meet) at the Airport.

6 She told her maid, "This room wouldn't need sweeping today if it (sweep) properly yesterday." Does the room need sweeping today? Was it swept properly yesterday?

7 It was a very nice house, and I might have bought it myself if it (not sell) a week ago.

8 He couldn't have sold his secondhand car if the engine (not repair). Could he sell his secondhand car? Was the engine repaired?

9 Very few Englishmen would know much about Tolstoi unless his books (translate) into English.

10 I don't think Yusef would have passed the examination unless he (give) extra lessons. Did Yusef pass the examination? Was he given extra lessons?

B Use the passive form of the Perfect Conditional tense of the verbs in brackets.

(a) Use: *would have been* + Part 3

1 If the thief had been caught, I am sure he (send) to prison for at least five years.

2 Fortunately it was only a slight earthquake. If it had been more severe, a lot of buildings (destroy).

3 Mary was rude to the teacher, but if she had apologised she (not punish) so severely.

4 If the murderer had not left his fingerprints on the revolver, he (not catch).

5 A fire broke out in a cinema. If the firemen hadn't come quickly, the cinema (burn) to the ground.

(b) Use: *might have been* + Part 3

6 The boy (drown) if he had fallen into the river.

7 I (bite) if I had trodden on the snake.

8 If you had found the stolen money, you (give) a very big reward.

9 The little girl ran across the road without looking. She (run over) and killed.

10 He was fined £50 for dangerous driving, but he (send) to prison.

(c) Use: *could have been* + Part 3

11 If the taxi-driver had put on his brakes, the accident (avoid).

12 It was a very large class, and the teacher spoke quietly. If he had spoken in a very loud voice, he (hear) by everyone.

13 If an Englishman had stolen a few pence two hundred years ago, he (hang).

14 He died yesterday, but some doctors thought he (cure) if he had had an operation six months ago.

15 The work (finish) yesterday if the workmen hadn't gone home early.

C Put the verbs in brackets into the Past Perfect tense (active OR passive) or the Perfect Conditional tense (active OR passive). Answer the questions which follow some of the sentences.

(a) Begin the Perfect Conditional tenses with *would*:

1 He cheated in the examination. He (expel) if he (catch) cheating.
Was he expelled? Was he caught cheating?

2 There (not be) a bus strike last year if the bus-drivers (give) higher wages.

3 If the clerk (not insult) the manager, he (not dismiss).
Did the clerk insult the manager? Was the clerk dismissed?

4 I helped an old lady across the road, but she didn't thank me. If someone (help) me, I (say) thank you.

5 If he (be) a good business man, he (not lose) all his money.

6 It was very hot and dry last summer. The grass in our garden (get) brown if it (not water) every day.

(b) Begin the Perfect Conditional tenses with *might*:

7 Mahmoud was lonely and often homesick when he was studying in London. If he (join) a club, he (make) more friends.

8 During the war, thousands of children were sent away from London. If they (stay) in London, they (kill) in the air raids. Did these children stay in London? Were they killed in the air raids on London?

9 The little boy was playing with his father's razor. He (cut) himself if his father (not take) the razor away from him.

10 I wasn't invited to the party. I (go) if I (invite).

11 If the prisoner (try) to escape, he (shoot). Did the prisoner try to escape? Was he shot?

12 He drove much too fast. He (have) an accident if there (be) a lot of traffic on the road.

(c) Begin the Perfect Conditional tenses with *could*:

13 She bought a pair of shoes which were too small for her, but she wore them for a fortnight. If she (take) them back to the shop without wearing them she (change) them for a bigger pair.

14 He (buy) a car last year if he (save) another £100.

15 If the book (write) in simple language, it (understand) by many more people.
Was the book written in simple language? Was it understood by many people?

16 He was a good chess player, but I (beat) him if I (not make) one bad move.

17 The little girl fell into the river and was drowned.
She (save) if a good swimmer (be) there at the time.

18 He (pass) the examination easily if he (take) it. Did he pass the examination? Did he take it?

Observation 6

Sentences from Exercises 1, 2, and 3 of Chapter 6

Which is the correct preposition to put in each space: *at*, *in*, or *on*?

1. The old man hasn't got enough money to live ———. If he'd saved more when he was young, he wouldn't be ——— need of help now.
2. I wouldn't buy a secondhand car unless I was sure the engine was ——— good condition.
3. If I'd known you were coming by the 6 p.m. train, I could have met you ——— the station.
4. She told the maid, "This room isn't clean. If you'd swept it properly, there wouldn't be so much dust ——— the floor."
5. He wasted his time ——— the university.
6. I think we could have won the football match if we'd played a little better ——— the second half.
7. Mr. Jones told his wife, "We could have a car if we hadn't spent so much ——— new furniture."
8. Jack said, "If I listened to the teacher more carefully, I might make fewer mistakes ——— dictation."
9. I wouldn't have believed the news unless I'd heard it ——— the wireless.
10. He looked ——— his watch while he was driving and thought, "If I hadn't stopped to get petrol, I might be home now."

Use the right part of speech, adjective, adverb, or noun, formed from the words in brackets. (Sentences from Exercises 4 and 5.)

1. He was fined £50 for (danger) driving, but he might have been sent to prison.
2. He could have passed the examination (easy) if he'd taken it.
3. No, I didn't watch television last night. I would have done so if I hadn't been reading a very (interest) book.
4. Mary was rude to the teacher, but if she had apologised she wouldn't have been punished so (severe).
5. If she'd been smoking there might have been an (explode).
6. If the (murder) had not left his fingerprints on the revolver, he wouldn't have been caught.
7. (Fortune) it stopped snowing some hours ago.

8 If the earthquake had been more severe, a lot of (build) would have been destroyed.

9 The sick man might have died if he hadn't been taken to hospital (immediate).

10 The little girl fell into the river and was drowned. She could have been saved if a good (swim) had been there at the time.

7 Should have + Part 3 and Similar Verb Forms

1 We learnt in Book 3 that *should* is commonly used to express duty, and that it does not refer to past time, for example:

> A man *should* help his parents when they become old.
> She has a very bad cold; she *shouldn't* go out.

In many cases when *should* is used, 'duty' is perhaps too strong a word, for example:

> George hasn't got very good eyesight; he *should* sit in the front of the class, near the blackboard.
> He has a bad cough; he *shouldn't* smoke so many cigarettes.

In the first sentence, *should* means that it would be better, or more sensible, if George sat near the blackboard. In the second sentence, *shouldn't* means that it would be better for the man's health, or that he would be more sensible, if he smoked fewer cigarettes.

Now read these sentences:

> (a) I *should have paid* this bill a month ago, but I hadn't enough money.
> (b) This bill *should have been paid* a month ago.

Both sentences refer to a past time (a month ago), to a past duty which was NOT done. I did NOT pay this bill. This bill was NOT paid.

> (c) The eggs were quite fresh; the servant *shouldn't have thrown* them away.
> (d) The eggs *shouldn't have been thrown* away.

These two sentences also refer to the past. The servant threw away the eggs, or the eggs were thrown away, but it was wrong to do so.

The formation of these verbs is:
Active: should, shouldn't have + Part 3 (paid, thrown)
Passive: should, shouldn't have been + Part 3 (paid, thrown)

Exercise 1

Use the active (should, shouldn't have + Part 3) OR the passive formation (should, shouldn't have been + Part 3) of the verbs in brackets.

1. Mary was feeling unwell yesterday; she (not go) to school.
2. I (send) him a birthday card, but I forgot to.
3. The Minister left some important papers on his desk; they (put) in a safer place.
4. The pupil didn't mean to be rude; the teacher (not be) so angry with him.
5. He is only seven years old and he needs his mother; he (not send) to a boarding-school.
6. It's three o'clock and I'm feeling very hungry; I (eat) more for lunch.
7. Henry wrote the answers in pencil; they (write) in ink.
8. He paid £20 for that watch, and it wasn't worth £10; he (not buy) it.
9. She went out and got caught in the rain; she (take) an umbrella with her.
10. The little boy was playing with his father's typewriter and of course he broke it; he (not allow) to play with it.
11. The old man ran to catch the bus, although he had a weak heart. He (not run).
12. She washed her new woollen dress in boiling water, and it shrank; it (wash) in warm, not boiling water.
13. The doctor said, "I'm sorry I'm late. I (be) here an hour ago, but I had a puncture."
14. He was only twenty-five and he (not give) such an important job, but his father was friendly with the director.
15. I was very tired last summer and I (take) a holiday, but there was too much work to do.
16. She spent the money her husband gave her on clothes, but it (spend) on food for the children.
17. When he went into his bedroom, he found it icy cold; he (not leave) the windows open.
18. This story is quite untrue; it (not print) in the newspapers.
19. I can't remember what he said; I (listen) more carefully.
20. The workmen are very slow; the job (finish) a week ago.

Note to the teacher: Make sure that pupils understand the *meaning*, by sometimes asking questions, for example after No. 1: Did Mary go to school yesterday? Was this a sensible thing to do?

The verb *ought*, followed by *to*, could be used instead of *should* in the above exercise, for example:

1. Mary was feeling unwell yesterday; she *ought not to have gone* to school. (Short form *oughtn't* – one word)
2. The Minister left some important papers on his desk; they *ought to have been put* in a safer place.

The formation is:

Active: ought, oughtn't to have + Part 3
Passive: ought, oughtn't to have been + Part 3

Exercise: Say or write the other sentences of the above exercise, using *ought to* instead of *should*.

2 If you see a man in the street tearing up pound notes and throwing the pieces into the air, you will probably say:

> He must be mad.

This sentence means that you, the speaker, are sure, or almost sure, that he is mad.

If you tell this story later, you will say:

> I saw a man in the street yesterday tearing up pound notes and throwing the pieces into the air. He *must have been* mad.

You mean: I am sure that he *was* mad.

Here are other examples, with the meanings in brackets:

1. My keys are not in any of my pockets. I *must have left* them at home. (I am sure, or almost sure, that I left them at home.)
2. I telephoned the doctor, but there was no reply. He *must have gone* out. (I am sure, or almost sure, that he had gone out.)
3. I can't find the newspaper anywhere. It *must have been thrown* away. (I am sure, or almost sure, that the newspaper was thrown away.)
4. I can't believe that no-one saw the thief; he *must have been*

seen by someone. (I am sure, or almost sure, that he was seen by someone.)

The formation of these verbs is:

Active (Sentences 1 and 2): must have + Part 3 (left, gone)
Passive (Sentences 3 and 4): must have been + Part 3 (thrown, seen)

Exercise 2

Use the active (must have + Part 3) OR the passive formation (must have been + Part 3) of the verbs in brackets.

1 I don't know at what time I went to bed last night, but it was late. It (be) after midnight.
2 It's an old house. It (built) at least seventy-five years ago.
3 When she came out of hospital, she looked the picture of health. She (look after) very well in hospital.
4 He promised to come at six o'clock, but he didn't. He (forget) his promise.
5 I didn't hear the telephone. I (be) asleep.
6 He never got the letter. It (send) to the wrong address.
7 When he spoke to the little girl, she ran away. She (frighten).
8 I can't remember the book, but I (read) it years ago.
9 He was a young man but when he came out of prison, his hair was white. He (treat) very badly in prison.
10 When I saw her, she was wearing a new fur coat. She (pay) a lot of money for it.
11 We looked everywhere, but we couldn't find the money. It (steal).
12 Why didn't you answer the question? You (know) the answer.
13 How did the thieves get into the bank at night? They (have) keys.
14 I should have got the letter this morning; it (post) yesterday.
15 The streets were very wet when I went out this morning; it (rain) hard during the night.
16 When the bomb exploded, the noise of the explosion (hear) a mile away.
17 Although the detectives searched the house from top to

bottom, they couldn't find the revolver, but it (hide) somewhere in the house.
18 The baby woke up when she went into the bedroom. She (make) a noise.
19 The taxi-driver got to the airport in half an hour. He (drive) very fast.
20 Henry was an hour late for the English examination. He said he didn't know the time of the examination, but he (tell).

3 *need not* (*needn't*) means 'it is not necessary' in sentences like the following:

> The teacher has just bought a car, so he *needn't* walk to school every day.

Read these sentences:

> The clerk must be in his office at nine o'clock, but he got up yesterday at six. He *needn't have got* up so early.

This means: it was not necessary for the clerk to get up at six o'clock, but he did so. We often continue in this way:

> He *could have stayed* in bed for another hour.

This means: it was possible for the clerk to stay in bed for another hour, but he didn't.

The formation of these verbs is:

> needn't have + Part 3 (got)
> could have + Part 3 (stayed)

Note to the teacher: The verb *need* can also have a regular negative form, for example: The teacher has just bought a car, so he *doesn't need to* walk to school every day. This has the same meaning as 'he needn't walk'. But the irregular and regular Past tense negative forms may give different meanings:

He needn't have got up so early (but he *did* get up).
He didn't need to get up so early (and he *didn't*).

Students should use the irregular or regular past negative forms to express such different meanings as in the above two sentences; but they should note that the regular form can express the meaning in this sentence: I didn't really need to take a taxi, but I had plenty of money in my pocket, so I did.

Exercise 3

Add two sentences to each of the following, (1) needn't have + Part 3, (2) could have + Part 3. Use the words given after each sentence, for example:

> He got to the station half an hour before the train left. 1. take a taxi. 2. walk.
>
> Answer: 1. He *needn't have taken* a taxi. 2. He *could have walked.*

1. His shirt was quite clean. 1. change it. 2. wear it for another day or two.
2. The bread was only a day old. 1. we ——— throw it away. 2. we ——— eat it.
3. The watch cost £50. 1. he ——— pay so much. 2. he ——— buy a cheaper one.
4. Mary had only a very slight cold. 1. she ——— be absent yesterday. 2. she ——— come to school.
5. It was a warm sunny day. 1. the old man ——— stay indoors. 2. he ——— sit in the garden.
6. I got his letter yesterday, saying he was coming to see me. 1. he ——— write. 2. he ——— phone.
7. Mr. Smith wasn't hungry. 1. his wife ——— cook a big meal. 2. she ——— make a few sandwiches.
8. Ahmad's father has got a very good English dictionary. 1. Ahmad ——— buy one. 2. He ——— use his father's.
9. He retired in 1955, when he was sixty. 1. he ——— retire in 1955. 2. he ——— go on working until he was sixty-five.
10. Her suitcase was very light. 1. she ——— give it to a porter. 2. she ——— carry it herself.
11. It didn't rain all day. 1. I ——— take my umbrella. 2. I ——— leave it at home.
12. Mary's homework was very easy. 1. her father ——— help her. 2. she ——— do it without any help.

13 The letter was not important. 1. you —— keep it. 2. you —— tear it up.
14 The young man had to pay a debt of £200. 1. he —— sell his car. 2. he —— borrow the money from his father.
15 The bus was full, but I jumped on. 1. I —— do so. 2. I —— wait for the next bus.
16 The police questioned him for several hours. 1. he —— answer their questions. 2. he —— refuse to say anything.
17 There were plenty of empty seats. 1. we —— stand. 2. we —— sit down.
18 Yusef asked the teacher, "What's the meaning of this word?" 1. he —— ask the teacher. 2. he —— find the meaning in his dictionary.
19 The carpenter worked yesterday, although it was a public holiday. 1. he —— work. 2. he —— have a day off.
20 There was a play on television last night, but Jack didn't enjoy it. 1. he —— watch it. 2. he —— turn off the set.

Note to the teacher: Make sure that pupils understand the *meaning* of the sentences they add, by sometimes asking questions, for example after No. 5: Did the old man stay indoors? Yes, he did. Did he sit in the garden? No, he didn't.

Notice the passive form in this sentence:

> I paid the bill in October, but it *needn't have been paid* until the end of the year.

Exercise 4

Use the passive form (needn't have been + Part 3) of the verbs in brackets.

1 The water was clean and fit to drink; it (boil).
2 She washed all the plates, but some of them had not been used; they (wash).
3 Ahmad answered all the questions in the examination, but two of the questions (answer).
4 Some pupils learnt the poem by heart, but the teacher told the class only to read it at home. It (learn) by heart.
5 I knew I had to be at the airport before ten o'clock; I (tell).

6 Jack was wide awake when his mother called him at seven o'clock this morning; he (call).

7 The servant swept the floor in the morning and swept it again in the afternoon; it (sweep) twice.

8 The letter wasn't very important; it (register).

9 The gardener planted the flowers in March, but they (plant) until May.

10 Why did the workmen paint the garage doors? They were painted a few months ago. They (paint) again.

Exercise 5

Put each verb between brackets into the right one of these forms:

> should (shouldn't) have + Part 3
> needn't have + Part 3
> could have + Part 3
> must have + Part 3

1 When Mrs. Brown came home yesterday after doing some shopping, she found that the butcher had given her short change. He (make) a mistake, but she (count) her change. She (not leave) the shop without making sure she had the right change.

2 Mr. Jones was in no hurry, but he flew from London to New York. He (not go) by plane; he (take) a ship from Southampton. The voyage takes only five days.

3 When the bell rang at the end of the lesson, Jack hadn't finished the exercise. The teacher looked at his book, and said, "You (finish) ten minutes ago. Why did you write the questions? You (not write) them. I told the class to write the answers only. You (hear) me tell you."

4 After the examination last summer, Ahmad became ill. He (study) too hard. He (not do) so, for he was an excellent student, and I'm sure he (pass) easily without working so hard.

5 The doctor said to himself, "I wish I had taken a holiday a month ago. I wasn't so busy then, and I (have) a holiday. I (listen) to my wife, who wanted us to go away for a fortnight."

6 Mary went to school yesterday, although it was a public holiday. The teacher (tell) her there was a holiday, but Mary (forget). She (not go) to school; she (stay) at home and helped her mother in the house.

7 The bus was full, and when a very old lady got on, she had to stand. There was a young man sitting near her, but he didn't get up. He (offer) her his seat; he (not let) an old lady stand. He (know) it was not polite or kind to sit while a very old lady was standing.

8 He was very angry with his little boy, and gave him a severe beating. His wife said to him later, "You (not beat) him so severely. I know he (not be) so naughty, but he's too young to be beaten. You (tell) him not to be naughty. I'm sure that would have been enough."

Observation 7

Sentences from the first 4 exercises of Chapter 7

Is it right to put *the*, *a*, *an*, OR NO Article in the spaces:

1 When she came out of hospital, she looked ——— picture of ——— health.

2 There was ——— play on television ——— last night, but Jack didn't enjoy it.

3 She spent the money her husband gave her on ——— clothes, but it should have been spent on ——— food for ——— children.

4 Mary had only ——— very slight cold.

5 Some pupils learnt the poem by ——— heart, but ——— teacher told ——— class to read it at ——— home.

6 The old man ran to catch the bus, although he had ——— weak heart.

7 I don't know at what time I went to ——— bed last night, but it was late. It must have been after ——— midnight.

8 Why did the workmen paint ——— garage doors? They were painted ——— few months ago.

9 Henry wrote the answers in ——— pencil; they should have been written in ——— ink.

10 The streets were very wet when I went out this morning; it must have rained hard during ——— night.

11 ——— bread was only ——— day old. We needn't have thrown it away.

12 She went out and got caught in ——— rain; she should have taken ——— umbrella with her.

Use the right part of speech, adjective, adverb, or noun, formed from the words in brackets.

1 It was a warm (sun) day.
2 She washed her new (wool) dress in (boil) water, and it shrank.
3 Jack was wide (wake) when his mother called him at seven o'clock this morning.
4 Although the (detect) searched the house from top to bottom, they couldn't find the revolver.
5 When he went into his bedroom, he found it (ice) cold.
6 I can't remember what he said; I should have listened more (careful).
7 He was only twenty-five, and he shouldn't have been given such an important job, but his father was (friend) with the director.

8 Have to

1 *must* is a defective verb, with only this one part, which is used to speak about the present time or a near future, as in these sentences: I must answer this letter at once; I must get up early tomorrow.

Because *must* is defective, another verb is needed which can be used in all tenses. This verb is *have to*, followed by Part 1, and here are examples of its use:

> Present tense: She *has to* wear glasses, but only for reading.
> Past tense: The last bus had gone, so we *had to* take a taxi.

Note to the teacher: It is right to use *must* in dependent clauses when the principal verb is in the Past tense, for example:

His mother often *told* him (when he was a little boy) that he *must* always tell the truth.

> Future tense: If you go to Russia next winter, you *will have to* take some warm clothes with you.
>
> Present Perfect tense: James *has had to* walk to school since he sold his bicycle.
>
> Past Perfect tense: The old man said that he *had had to* work very hard all his life.
>
> Conditional tense: If you were a teacher of English, you *would have to* correct a lot of exercise-books.
>
> Perfect Conditional tense: If I hadn't caught the last train, I *would have had to* stay the night in a hotel.

2 Negative forms of *have to* followed by Part 1 are as follows:

> Present tense: We *don't have to* come to school on Fridays (or Sundays).
>
> She *doesn't have to* wear glasses, except for reading.

These negatives do NOT have the same meaning as *must not*:

> We *don't have to* come to school. (It is NOT necessary)
> We *mustn't* play in class. (It is NOT allowed)

Note to the teacher: It is right to use *mustn't* (not allowed) in dependent clauses when the principal clause is in the Past tense, for example:

The teacher *told* us (that) we *mustn't* play in class.
The little boy *knew* he *mustn't* pull his sister's hair.

Past tense:	She had three servants, so she *didn't have to* do any housework.
Future tense:	The doctor said, "You're much better. You *won't have to* go to hospital."
Present Perfect tense:	I *haven't had to* buy a book since I joined the library.
Past Perfect tense:	She told me she *hadn't had to* buy a new dress since 1963.
Conditional tense:	If I were a rich man, I *wouldn't have to* work.
Perfect Conditional tense:	If his father had lent him the money, he *wouldn't have had to* borrow from the bank.

Exercise 1

Fill in the spaces with one of the following 6 verbs:
has to – have to – don't have to – doesn't have to – had to – didn't have to

Your sense will tell you whether to use the Present or Past tense, and when to use the negative forms.

1 I ——— write some letters before I go to bed tonight.
2 Fifty years ago, labourers ——— work very long hours.
3 He's a rich man; he ——— work.
4 The plane takes off at 11 a.m. She ——— be at the airport at 10.30 a.m.
5 Fortunately his wife could drive, so he ——— drive all the way himself.
6 The apples were rotten; we ——— throw them away.
7 You can finish the work tomorrow; you ——— finish it today.
8 Ahmad ——— pass two more examinations before he becomes a doctor.

Have to 81

9 Yesterday was a holiday, so we ——— get up early.
10 English children ——— start school when they are five years old.
11 It's too early to leave the house. It's only nine o'clock. We ——— be at the station before ten.
12 When his father died, he ——— leave school and find a job.
13 Jack's father has to get up at seven on weekdays, but he ——— get up early on Sundays.
14 The old man can't go out when it's cold. He ——— stay indoors during the winter.
15 Ahmad lent me his dictionary, so I ——— buy one.
16 Mr. and Mrs. Wilson have three young children, and they ——— save money for their education.
17 If you don't like the film, you ——— stay in the cinema until the end.
18 Millions of young men ——— join the army during the last war.
19 She lives a long way from the shops, but fortunately she ——— go shopping every day.
20 The bus was half empty yesterday, so I ——— stand.
21 Her father doesn't allow her to stay out late. She ——— be in by nine o'clock every evening.
22 He told the police officer, "I ——— answer your questions, but I will."
23 I must go to bed early tonight, as I ——— catch a train at five o'clock tomorrow morning.
24 The clerk usually gets to the office at 8.30 a.m. but he ——— begin work until 9 a.m.
25 He retired when he was sixty, although he ———.

Exercise 2

Fill in the spaces with one of the following 4 verbs. Practise using both the full form and the short form in brackets.

will ('ll) have to – will not (won't) have to
would ('d) have to – would not (wouldn't) have to

1 Her coat is very shabby. She ——— buy a new one next winter.

Lesson 8

2 If he had a secretary, he ——— type his letters himself.
3 If there is another war, Henry's father ——— join the army again. He'll be too old.
4 The old man told his sons that they ——— depend on themselves when he was dead.
5 He has missed the train; he ——— wait for the next one.
6 If she had a car, she ——— walk to the shops every day.
7 I'm very pleased that tomorrow is a holiday. I ——— get up early.
8 If she became a nurse, she ——— work sometimes all night.
9 He's fifty-five, and he ——— retire when he's sixty. That is the rule.
10 If she had a nurse for the children, she ——— look after them herself.
11 The doctor said, "You're much better today. You ——— go to hospital."
12 If Jack's father lost his job, Jack ——— leave school and start work.
13 My shirt is dirty. I ——— put on a clean one tomorrow morning.
14 I was told that entrance to the museum was free, and that I ——— pay anything.
15 If you borrowed money from the bank, you ——— pay interest on it.
16 I am going in my friend's car; I ——— take my own car.
17 The manager told the new clerk that he'd have to work on Saturday mornings, but he ——— work in the afternoons.
18 I can't understand this book; I ——— read it again.
19 Yusef often made careless mistakes. The teacher told him that he ——— be more careful.
20 The old man and his wife are going to move soon into a ground floor flat, and then they ——— climb up and down stairs.
21 She's living in India now, where servants are cheap, but when she returns to England, she ——— do without servants.
22 If I couldn't move the cupboard myself, I ——— ask someone to help me.
23 He knows the way from the station to my house; I ——— meet him at the station.

24 The teacher was angry with the class and said, "If you listened more carefully, I —— explain everything twice."

Exercise 3

Fill in the spaces with one of the following 6 verbs. Practise using both the full form and the short form in brackets.

> have ('ve) had to – has ('s) had to – had ('d) had to
> haven't had to – hasn't had to – hadn't had to

1 He can't afford a new suit; he —— wear the same suit for five years.

2 Mary —— walk to school since her father gave her a bicycle.

3 He told me that he —— stop smoking since his last illness.

4 I wasn't feeling well yesterday. If I —— go out, I'd have stayed in bed all day.

5 I've been very busy this month; I —— work until ten o'clock every night.

6 Mrs. Smith told her neighbour, "We are very pleased with our fridge; we —— throw away any food since we bought it."

7 I had to take a taxi; I wouldn't have done so unless I ——.

8 He —— get up early since he took a new job; the office is an hour's bus ride from his home.

9 The old man said he —— earn his living since he was fourteen years old.

10 She —— sweep the carpets since she bought a vacuum cleaner.

11 He said, "Fortunately my teeth are very good. I —— visit a dentist since 1955."

12 When the doctor returned home in the morning, he told his wife that he —— stay all night in the hospital.

13 If Henry —— take the examination last year, I think he would have failed.

14 The poor old man has no-one to look after him. He —— look after himself since his wife died.

15 He told me he had saved enough money to buy a house, and that he —— borrow from anyone.

16 It's been raining hard since we got up this morning; we —— stay indoors all day.

17 He ——— get up early since he retired last year; he can stay in bed until noon if he wants to.
18 Ahmad said, "I ——— stop playing football since I broke my leg."
19 He was a clever boy, but his family were poor. If he ——— leave school when his father died, he'd have gone to a university.
20 Her eyesight is weak. She ——— wear glasses since she was four years old.
21 They have a lot of furniture. They ——— buy any new furniture since they got married.
22 When I asked him, he told me he ——— wait long for a bus, only a few minutes.
23 She ——— work so hard since she found a servant.
24 I've made so many mistakes in this exercise that I ——— do it again.

Exercise 4

Fill in the spaces with either:

would have had to OR wouldn't have had to

Practise using the short forms also:

I'd (He'd etc.) 've had to OR wouldn't 've had to

1 Fortunately I found the book I had borrowed from the library. If I hadn't found it, I ——— buy a new one.
2 If Mahmoud had failed last year, he ——— take the examination again.
3 She was a very extravagant young woman. If she hadn't spent so much money, her father ——— help her.
4 We were late and we found the cinema crowded. If we had got there earlier, we ——— wait for seats.
5 The teacher told George, "If you hadn't told me the truth, I ——— punish you."
6 If there had been a holiday yesterday, we ——— come to school.
7 If Mary had got up earlier this morning, she ——— run all the way to school.

8 His family was very rich and he did nothing. If his family had been poor, he ——— work for his living.

9 If all the class had listened carefully, the teacher ——— explain everything twice.

10 If his father hadn't lost all his money in business, the young man ——— leave the university.

11 If no-one had helped me, I ——— do the job myself.

12 Mr. and Mrs. Brown went by car from London to Edinburgh, but Mrs. Brown hadn't passed her driving test, so she couldn't drive. If she had passed the test, Mr. Brown ——— drive all the way himself.

13 He was out of work for six months and then he found a good job. If he hadn't taken that job, he ——— sell his car.

14 The last bus had gone. If there had been another bus, I ——— take a taxi.

15 Jack was a boy at school during the 1939–45 war. If he had been a young man, he ——— join the army.

3 The correct answers to the first five sentences of Exercise 1 were:

1 I *have to* write some letters before I go to bed tonight.

2 Fifty years ago, labourers *had to* work very long hours.

3 He's a rich man; he *doesn't have to* work.

4 The plane takes off at 11 a.m. She *has to* be at the airport at 10.30 a.m.

5 Fortunately his wife could drive, so he *didn't have to* drive all the way himself.

There is another verb form which could be used to give these answers:

1 I*'ve got to* write some letters before I go to bed tonight.

2 Fifty years ago, labourers *had got to* work very long hours.

3 He's a rich man; he *hasn't got to* work.

4 The plane takes off at 11 a.m. She*'s (has) got to* be at the airport at 10.30 a.m.

5 Fortunately his wife could drive, so he *hadn't got to* drive all the way himself.

This verb form is perhaps more common in speech than in writing, and it is used ONLY in the Present and Past tenses.

Exercise 5

Repeat Sentences 6–25 of Exercise 1, filling in the spaces with one of the following forms. Use both the full and the short form in brackets.

> has ('s) got to – have ('ve) got to
> hasn't got to   – haven't got to
> had ('d) got to – hadn't got to

4 Questions using *have to* or *have got to*, followed by Part 1, are asked in this way:

> Present tense: At what time *do* you *have to* leave home in the morning?
>
> *Does* your father *have to* wear glasses?
>
> *Have* you *got to* walk home, or can you take a bus?
>
> *Has* your mother *got to* cook every day?
>
> Past tense: *Did* you *have to* go to bed early when you were a child?

Note: The Past tense question form *Had* ——— *got to* ———? is not very common.

> Future tense: *Will* you *have to* earn your own living when you finish your education?
>
> Present Perfect tense: *Have* you *had to* go to a dentist this year?
>
> *Has* the teacher ever *had to* punish you?

Notice the position in the question of *ever*.

> Conditional tense: If you were a teacher, *would* you *have to* work hard?
>
> Perfect Conditional tense: If he hadn't caught the last train yesterday, *would* he *have had to* stay the night in a hotel?

Exercise 6

Make questions to which the following sentences are full answers. Be careful to use the same tense in the question as in the sentence.

1 No, we haven't got to do homework every evening.

Have to

2 Yes, the little girl will have to start school soon.
3 Yes, I'd (I would) have to live in the capital if I was a Minister.
4 No, I didn't have to take a taxi.
5 No, he's never had to borrow money. (Use *ever* in the question.)
6 No, I don't have to clean my own shoes.
7 He's got to pass two more examinations before he becomes a doctor. (Begin the question: How many more ———)
8 I'd have had to wait an hour if I hadn't caught that bus. (Begin the question: How long ———)
9 I had to get up yesterday at 5 a.m. (Begin the question: At what time ———)
10 No, I wouldn't have to walk to school if I had a bicycle.
11 Yes, the old man has to stay indoors during the winter.
12 She's had to wear that old coat for five years. (Begin the question: How long ———)
13 No, I won't have to pay this bill immediately.
14 Jack's father has to shave twice a day. (Begin the question: How often ———)
15 No, the teacher wouldn't have had to shout if the class had made less noise.
16 Yes, I've got to catch the first train tomorrow.
17 We have to write our corrections three times. (Begin the question: How many times ———)
18 I'd have to learn German if I went to a German university.
19 No, he's never had to work hard. (Use *ever* in the question.)
20 I'd have had to stand if someone hadn't offered me a seat.
21 The doctor has had to visit her every day this month. (Begin the question: How often ———)
22 No, she won't have to go to a university if she becomes a nurse.
23 We've had to study hard this year.
24 No, she hasn't got to go shopping every day.
25 No, I didn't have to wait a long time.
26 No, I wouldn't have had to buy a new watch if I hadn't lost my old one.
27 Henry had to drink a lot of milk when he was a little boy.

28 No, I've never had to go without food. (Use *ever* in the question.)
29 No, I won't have to buy a new suit this year.
30 I had to finish the work yesterday. (Begin the question: When ———)
31 No, she hasn't had to go to a dentist since 1960.
32 Yes, I've often had to travel all night. (Use *ever* in the question.)

Observation 8

Sentences from Exercises 1, 2, 3, and 4 of Chapter 8

Of each 2 words in brackets, which is the right one:

1 The old man said he'd had to earn his (life, living) since he was fourteen years old.
2 Ahmad (borrowed, lent) me his dictionary, so I didn't have to buy one.
3 He has (lost, missed) the train; he'll have to wait for the next one.
4 His family was very rich and he (did, made) nothing.
5 Her father doesn't (allow, let) her to stay out late.
6 He's had to get up early since he took a new (job, work); the office is an hour's bus ride from his home.
7 If you (borrowed, lent) money from the bank, you'd have to pay interest on it.
8 He can't afford a new (dress, suit); he's had to wear the same (dress, suit) for five years.
9 When his father (dead, died), he had to leave school and find a (job, work).
10 I've (done, made) so many mistakes in this exercise that I've had to (do, make) it again.
11 Fortunately I found the book I had (borrowed, lent) from the library.
12 It's been raining (hard, hardly) since we got up this morning.

Put the correct prepositions in the spaces:

1 I was told that entrance ——— the museum was free, and that I wouldn't have to pay anything.

2 Mr. and Mrs. Wilson have three young children, and they have to save money ——— their education.

3 Mrs. Smith told her neighbour, "We are very pleased ——— our fridge."

4 If his family had been poor, he'd have had to work ——— his living.

5 When I asked him, he told me he hadn't had to wait long ——— a bus, only a few minutes.

6 The teacher was angry ——— the class.

7 The old man told his sons that they'd have to depend ——— themselves when he was dead.

8 If she had a nurse ——— the children, she wouldn't have to look after them herself.

9 Be able to

1 *can* is also a defective verb, with only two forms: *can* and *could*. We therefore need another verb, for use in tenses which cannot be formed with *can* or *could*. This verb is:

> be able (unable) to + Part 1

The Present and Past tenses are: am, is, are, was, were able (unable) to. It is first necessary to notice the different meanings expressed by *could* and *was, were able to*, shown in these sentences:

(a) The old man *could* read without glasses until he was over seventy.
(b) I hadn't time to finish the book, but I *was able to* read most of it.

could in Sentence (a) means only that it was *possible* for the old man to read without glasses; it expresses only his *ability* to read without glasses.

In Sentence (b), we are expressing more than ability. We are saying two things: I *could* read and I *did* read most of the book. We MUST use *was, were able to*, and NOT *could*, if we wish to express a past ability AND a past achievement. (Achievement means: something done, usually something which needs effort.)

Exercise 1

Complete the following sentences. In 8 of them, *was, were able to* MUST be used; in 7, *could* is correct.

1 He asked me to lend him £10. I hadn't got £10, but I ——— lend him £5, and he was grateful.
2 A good suit costs at least £30 today, but in 1925 you ——— buy a suit for much less.
3 The fishing boat sank, but fortunately the fisherman ——— swim to the shore.
4 Thirty years ago a student in London ——— live comfortably on £30 a month.

5 When he was a young man, he ───── walk twenty miles a day.

6 The woman ───── describe the pickpocket to the police; she told them he was a thin little man, wearing a dirty raincoat.

7 It was a fine day yesterday, so we ───── have a picnic, and we enjoyed it very much.

8 Travelling was much cheaper fifty years ago; you ───── go by sea from England to Egypt for £10.

9 The Minister suddenly felt ill, but he ───── finish his speech, although at the end he could hardly stand.

10 He spoke very little French when he left school, but he ───── understand the language.

11 I got to the station at 9.50 a.m. and ───── catch the 9.55 a.m. train. I was very pleased I didn't have to wait for the next train.

12 The sick man had a restless night, but he ───── sleep for an hour or two.

13 She ───── visit her friends every morning before she got married if she wanted to, but now she can't; she has too much to do in the house.

14 The town was full of visitors, and we didn't know where we would spend the night, but at last we ───── find two vacant rooms in a small hotel.

15 Before his illness, he ───── work fourteen hours a day if he had to.

2 The following tenses of *be able to* are necessary and useful:

Future: shall, will ('ll), shall not (shan't), will not (won't) be able to

> Ahmad *will be able to* speak English fluently if he goes to England for a year or two.
> He *won't be able to* sell his house unless he reduces the price.
> *Will* you *be able to* earn your own living when you are twenty-five?

Present Perfect: have ('ve), has ('s) been able to

> Mr. and Mrs. Smith want to buy a house, but they *haven't been able to* save enough money yet.
> He*'s been able to* swim since he was three years old.
> This is a very dull book. I've started to read it several times, but I*'ve* never *been able to* finish it.

Lesson 9

Past Perfect: had ('d) been able to

> The old man said that fortunately he'*d been able to* give all his children a good education.
> She wouldn't have got the job if she *hadn't been able to* type.

Exercise 2

Fill in the spaces with either: *shall, will ('ll) be able to*, OR *shall not (shan't), will not (won't) be able to*. Practise using the short forms.

1. When they buy a car, they ——— visit their friends more often.
2. I'm sorry, but I ——— come to your birthday party next week.
3. I saw a terrible bus accident in London years ago. I ——— never ——— forget it.
4. It's very cold, and the old man ——— go out until the weather gets warmer.
5. Why do you sit at the back of the class if you can't hear well? You ——— hear better if you sit in the front.
6. Do you think you ——— support yourself when you are twenty-one?
7. He's getting a very small salary. He ——— get married until he has a much better job.
8. I'm too busy to have a holiday this year, but I hope I ——— have a long holiday next year.
9. The train leaves at five o'clock tomorrow morning. We ——— catch it unless we get up very early.
10. He was working very hard before he became ill. He ——— work so hard when he comes out of hospital.
11. His family are poor, and he ——— go to a university unless he gets a scholarship.
12. Perhaps one day we ——— travel to the moon.
13. The little girl is still ill, but she's getting better. The doctor hopes she ——— go back to school after the summer holidays.
14. This is a very difficult problem. I'm afraid you ——— solve it without help.
15. The doctor is very busy; he ——— see any more patients today.

16 He ——— spend more time with his grandchildren when he retires the year after next.
17 Mr. Brown is learning Russian, but he doesn't think he ——— ever ——— speak the language well.
18 There's a new English teacher coming next year. We ——— understand him unless he speaks slowly.
19 She's looking for a servant. If she finds one, she ——— rest more.
20 Jack has hurt his knee, and he ——— play football next Saturday.

Exercise 3

Fill in the spaces with one of the following 6 verb forms. Use the full forms and the short forms in brackets.

have ('ve) been able to – haven't been able to
has ('s) been able to – hasn't been able to
had ('d) been able to – hadn't been able to

1 She plays the piano well. She ——— play since she was a little girl.
2 I asked him if he had read the book and if he ——— understand it.
3 He ——— play any games since his illness.
4 She told the doctor that she ——— sleep well for over a month and that she felt very tired.
5 He asked me, "How long ——— you ——— drive a car?"
6 I know my suit looks shabby, but I ——— buy a new one since 1962.
7 He wouldn't have lived in a village all his life if he ——— get a good job in a city.
8 The business man said, "I work hard. I ——— never ——— have more than a fortnight's holiday a year."
9 She ——— go out in the evenings since she had a baby. She has to stay in and look after the baby.
10 He fell into the sea. He would have been drowned if he ——— swim.
11 She ——— cook very well since she took cooking lessons.

12 I've got a very bad cold and cough. I ――― go out for a week.

13 He would have passed the examination if he ――― answer all the questions, but he couldn't answer two of them.

14 I answered his question and said, "I ――― drive a car since 1955."

15 He is very bad at arithmetic. He ――― never ――― add up correctly.

16 The old man and his wife are too old to live alone. They ――― look after themselves for more than two years.

17 The little girl ran across the road without looking. The bus would have knocked her down if the driver ――― stop in time.

18 Her husband is poor, and she ――― buy a new dress for three years.

19 The farmer said, "I like riding a horse. I ――― ride since I was a little boy."

20 The old man ――― walk without a stick since he fell down and broke his leg.

21 He didn't get the job. He would have got it if he ――― speak two foreign languages.

22 I visited my old friend two years ago, but I ――― visit him since then.

23 No, his father doesn't give him any money. He ――― support himself since he left the university.

24 Mary told the teacher she was sorry, but she ――― do all her homework.

3 In Chapter 6, we learnt the use in conditional sentences of could + Part 1, and of could have + Part 3. Here are completed sentences from the exercises in that chapter, in which these verbs are correctly used:

(a) If Jack's father gave him £20, he *could buy* a new bicycle.

(b) If you had bought a house in 1945 for £3000, you *could sell* it today for probably £6000.

(c) We *could have sent* them a Christmas card if we'd known their address.

(d) If you'd been learning English fifty years ago, you *couldn't have listened* to English by Radio.

Instead of using *could*, we can use the Conditional and Perfect Conditional tenses of *be able to*, and express these sentences as follows:

(a) If Jack's father gave him £20, he *would be able to* buy a bicycle.

(b) If you had bought a house in 1945 for £3000, you *would be able to* sell it today for probably £6000.

(c) We *would have been able to* send them a Christmas card if we'd known their address.

(d) If you'd been learning English fifty years ago, you *wouldn't have been able to* listen to English by Radio.

Exercise 4

Rewrite the following completed sentences from the exercises in Chapter 6, using *would (wouldn't) be able to* + Part 1, OR *would (wouldn't) have been able to* + Part 1.

1 We could understand the English teacher if he spoke more slowly.

2 Could you cook your own dinner if your mother was ill?

3 I think we could have won the football match if we'd played a little better in the second half.

4 I sat at the back of the theatre and couldn't hear very well. If I'd been sitting nearer the stage, I could have heard better.

5 He couldn't have sold his secondhand car if the engine hadn't been repaired.

6 James is rather short. If he was taller, he could wear his brother's clothes.

7 Mr. Jones told his wife, "We could have a car if we hadn't spent so much on new furniture."

8 Could you have answered these questions if you'd been absent for the last fortnight?

9 He could have passed the examination easily if he'd taken it.

10 I like reading, but I haven't much time. If I'd more time, I could read a lot more.

11 If Jack hadn't hurt his ankle yesterday, he could play football this afternoon.

12 If I'd known you were coming by the 6 p.m. train, I could have met you at the station.

13 Could you come to school an hour earlier tomorrow if the teacher asked you?

14 Fortunately it stopped snowing some hours ago. We couldn't have taken the car if it had still been snowing.

15 If Henry's father had had enough money in 1950, he could have bought a bigger house.

Observation 9

Sentences from Exercises 1, 2, and 3 of Chapter 9

Which is the right word to put in each space: *much*, *too*, or *very*?

1 I've got a ——— bad cold and cough.
2 Travelling was ——— cheaper fifty years ago; you could go by sea from England to Egypt for £10.
3 I was ——— pleased I didn't have to wait for the next train.
4 The old man and his wife are ——— old to live alone.
5 He won't be able to get married until he has a ——— better job.
6 She could visit her friends every morning before she got married if she wanted to, but now she can't; she has ——— much to do in the house.
7 She's been able to cook ——— well since she took cooking lessons.
8 The train leaves at five o'clock tomorrow morning. We won't be able to catch it unless we get up ——— early.
9 A good suit costs at least £30 today, but in 1925 you could buy a suit for ——— less.
10 I'm ——— busy to have a holiday this year, but I hope I'll be able to have a long holiday next year.

In each of the following sentences, ONE word is spelt incorrectly. Find and correct it.

1 He'd have past the examination if he'd been able to answer all the questions, but he couldn't answer two of them.
2 It's very cold, and the old man won't be able to go out untill the weather gets warmer.

3 The Minister suddenly felt ill, but he was able to finish his speech, although at the end he could hardly stand.
4 He didn't get the job. He would have got it if he'd been able to speak two foriegn languages.
5 The fishing boat sank, but fortunatly the fishermen were able to swim to the shore.
6 Jack has hurt his knee, and he won't be able to play football next Saturday.
7 It was a fine day yesterday, so we were able to have a picnic, and we enjoied it very much.
8 He is very bad at arithmatic.
9 The town was full of visiters.
10 The farmer said, "I like ridding a horse. I've been able to ride since I was a little boy."

10 Past Forms, but not Past Time

Part 2 of the verb is used in conditional sentences (see page 54), but it does NOT refer to past time in sentences like the following:

> If I *knew* the answer, I'd tell you.
> I would never drive a car unless it *was* insured.
> If we never *had* a holiday, we'd soon get tired of school.

The following are other common uses of Part 2 of the verb in which, although the form is past, the time referred to is not past.

1 Read these sentences. The words in brackets make their meaning fuller.

(a) I wish I *knew* how to drive a car. (At the time of speaking, the speaker doesn't know how to drive a car.)

or

I don't know how to drive a car. I wish I *did*.

(b) I wish I *lived* in the centre of the city. (At the time of speaking, the speaker doesn't live in the centre of the city.)

or

I don't live in the centre of the city. I wish I *did*.

(c) I wish today *was* a holiday. (But today is not a holiday.)

(d) I wish I *had* more time to read. (At the time of speaking, the speaker hasn't got much time to read.)

(e) I wish I *could* travel round the world. (At the time of speaking, the speaker can't travel round the world. Perhaps he hasn't got enough money, or time.)

(f) I'm sorry, but I can't come to the club with you this evening. I wish I *could*.

(g) The teacher said to John, "I wish you *would* take more care with your spelling." (John doesn't take care.)

(h) The father told his children, "I wish you *wouldn't* make so much noise. I've got a headache." (When the father says this, his children are making a lot of noise.)

In all these sentences, the present verb *wish* is followed by Part 2 (knew, did, lived, was, had, could, would, wouldn't), but these Part 2 forms do NOT refer to past time.

Past Forms, but not Past Time 99

Exercise 1

(a) Add to each of the following 2 sentences, both beginning: I wish ——— Choose the right one of these ways:

    1 I don't understand this question.
Answer: I wish I *did*. I wish I *understood* this question.

    2 I feel tired.
Answer: I wish I *didn't*. I wish I *didn't feel* tired.

    3 It's still raining.
Answer: I wish it *wasn't*. I wish it *wasn't* still raining.

    4 I'm not a good chess player.
Answer: I wish I *was*. I wish I *was* a good chess player.

    5 My father can't give me more pocket money.
Answer: I wish he *could*. I wish he *could* give me more pocket money.

    1 My father doesn't have a very long holiday.

    2 I can't play the piano.

    3 My tooth is aching.

    4 I sometimes make careless mistakes.

    5 He's not coming to see me today.

    6 I can't swim well.

    7 I don't know how to answer this question.

    8 The shops are shut. (Notice the *plural* verb.)

    9 My friend can't find a good job.

  10. It isn't time to go home.

  11 He always drives too fast.

  12 I don't speak English fluently.

  13 I can't go to the cinema this evening.

  14 I'm not rich.

  15 My best friend is leaving this school.

  16 The teacher gives us a lot of homework.

  17 My father doesn't come home from work early.

  18 There are no flowers in the garden. (Notice the *plural* verb.)

  19 I live a long way from the school.

  20 Our television set is broken.

  21 My little sister doesn't like school.

  22 I can't sell my old bicycle.

23 I don't sit near the blackboard.
24 Ahmad is ill.

(b) Express the following orders in another way, beginning: I wish you would (wouldn't), for example:

> Take more care. I wish you would take more care.
> Don't shout at me. I wish you wouldn't shout at me.

1 Don't throw rubbish on the floor.
2 Listen to me.
3 Use a dictionary.
4 Don't come into the room without knocking.
5 Don't waste so much time.
6 Try to answer my questions.
7 Get up earlier.
8 Don't be so impatient.
9 Don't ask foolish questions.
10 Look where you're going.
11 Speak more clearly.
12 Don't open the windows.
13 Don't walk so fast.
14 Write more carefully.
15 Don't wear that old suit any more.
16 Don't interrupt me.
17 Help me move this cupboard.
18 Don't talk while I am talking.
19 Don't be so untidy.
20 Keep quiet.

2 Study these sentences:

> It's nearly midnight. It's time the children *went* to bed.
> It's 3 p.m. and I haven't had anything to eat since breakfast. It's time I *had* lunch.

In these sentences, Part 2 of the verb (went, had) is used after *It's time*, although it clearly does NOT refer to past time. If we think it necessary to make the sentence 'stronger', we add the adjective 'high', for example:

> He borrowed some money from me five years ago, and he hasn't paid it back yet. It's *high* time he *paid* me back.

Exercise 2

Add a sentence to each of the following, beginning: It's time. If you think it necessary, begin: It's high time.

Example 1: I've only got one suit, and it's three years old.
Answer : It's time I *bought* a new suit.
Example 2: He's over seventy years old, and he's still working.
Answer : It's (high) time he *stopped* working.

1 It's 9 a.m. and Jack is still in bed.
2 She's nearly seven years old, but she hasn't started school yet.
3 He's very dirty; he hasn't had a bath for a month!
4 The doctor has been working for two years without a holiday.
5 I haven't had a haircut for over a month, and my hair is very long.
6 It's nearly one o'clock, and she hasn't begun to cook the lunch yet.
7 The poor man has been out of work for a year.
8 I wrote to him a fortnight ago, but he hasn't answered my letter.
9 He's fourteen years old and he still wears short trousers.
10 We've played ten football matches this year, but we haven't won a single game.
11 The doctor said, "You're smoking too many cigarettes."
12 His car is ten years old, and it's in very bad condition.
13 Mary hasn't answered one question in this lesson.
14 Mr. Thomson has been living in Spain for three years, but he hasn't learnt a word of Spanish.
15 It's not a difficult examination, but George has taken it four times and failed each time.

3 Read the following:

> When Mr. Jones came home from work, he said to his wife, "I've been very busy today. I'm feeling tired."
> His wife answered, "You'*d better go* to bed early, and you'*d better not work* so hard tomorrow."

His wife means: it would be better for you if you went to bed early, and it would be better for you if you did not work so hard tomorrow. She is giving her husband advice, and she expresses this advice in a very common way:

> had ('d) better (not) + Part 1 (go, work)

had is Part 2 of the verb *have*, but this is another case in which Part 2 does not refer to past time.

Here are other examples:

> I think it's going to rain. I'*d better take* my raincoat.
> He's getting very fat. He'*d better eat* less.
> We're late. We'*d better take* a taxi.
> Mr. and Mrs. Smith don't like flying. They'*d better go* by sea.

Exercise 3

Add a sentence of 'advice' to each of the following. The words in brackets are to help you, for example:

> I've got a very bad toothache. (dentist)
> *Answer:* You'd better go to (*or* see) a dentist.

(a) Begin your sentences with: You ——

1. There are a lot of difficult words in this book. (dictionary)
2. I can't see the blackboard. (at the front)
3. The train leaves at 7 a.m. tomorrow. (get up)
4. He won't get a letter in time. (a telegram)
5. I'm sorry, but I can't answer your question. (someone else)
6. It's getting dark. (put on)

(b) Begin your sentences with: I ——

1. He doesn't know the way from the station. (meet)
2. This letter is important. (register)

Past Forms, but not Past Time

3 My shirt is dirty. (clean, tomorrow)
4 You can't move this table by yourself. (help)
5 It's cold in this room. (windows)
6 The police are going to question me. (the truth)

(c) Begin your sentences with: They ———

1 Some students make a lot of careless mistakes. (more careful)
2 The house is much too big for them. (smaller)
3 Both he and his wife are very extravagant. (save)
4 Those children are shivering with cold. (their overcoats)
5 They won't be able to catch the ten o'clock train. (wait)
6 I think those people have lost their way. (policeman)

(d) Use in your sentences: had ('d) better not + Part 1.

1 He's got a very bad cough. He ——— (out)
2 Somebody may want this newspaper. You ——— (it away)
3 We've got a lot of homework this evening. We——— (cinema)
4 I want the truth. You ——— (lies)
5 Mary has been late for school every day this week.
  She ——— (late tomorrow)
6 This bag is very heavy. You ——— (yourself)
7 He has very bad eyesight. He ——— (car)
8 She has to get up very early tomorrow. She ——— (bed late)
9 It's cold in this room. We ——— (the windows)
10 Why didn't you bring your English book today? You ———
  (to bring it tomorrow)
11 This water is dirty. We ———
12 She has a lot of work to do tomorrow. She ——— (late)

4 We have learnt that *would*, *might*, and *could* are used in conditional sentences, for example:

> If I knew the answer, I *would* tell you.
> If I had £1000, I *could* buy a good car.
> If I didn't take care of my money, I *might* lose it.

In these sentences, *would, could,* and *might* do NOT refer to past time, although they are the past forms of *will, can,* and *may*.

There are other common uses of *would*, *could*, and *might*, in which these verbs have no past meaning.

(a) *would*

Read the following conversation between Mr. Robinson and a friend who is visiting him. They are in the sitting-room, after dinner.

> Mr. Robinson: *Would* you like to watch television, or *would* you prefer to listen to some gramophone records?
>
> Friend: I'*d* rather listen to some records. But I'm feeling a little cold. *Would* you mind closing a window?

The questions beginning with *Would* are polite. Notice the formation of the question:

> Would you mind + -ing

would ('*d*) *rather listen* means *would prefer to listen*. If we wish to make the full sentence, it is:

> I'd rather listen to some records *than* watch television.

The formation is:

> would ('d) rather + Part 1 (listen) than + Part 1 (watch)

It is not necessary to repeat the same Part 1 verb after *than*, for example:

> He'd rather be a doctor than an engineer.

Note to the teacher: *sooner* may be used instead of *rather*. It is also correct to say *had rather* or *sooner*, but *would* is perhaps more common.

Exercise 4

(a) Change these orders into polite requests, beginning: Would you mind (not) + -ing.

1 Say it again.
2 Don't make so much noise.
3 Shut the door.
4 Lend me your bicycle.
5 Don't stand in front of me. I can't see.
6 Post this letter for me.

Past Forms, but not Past Time

7 Don't park your car in front of my gate.
8 Speak more slowly.
9 Don't leave your books on your desks at the end of the lesson.
10 Carry one of my bags.
11 Don't drive so fast.
12 Knock at the door before you come in.

(b) Answer these questions fully, for example:

> Which would you prefer, to play chess or (to) go for a walk?
> I'd prefer to play chess than (to) go for a walk.

Notice that the second *to* is not necessary; it can be left out.

1 Which would you prefer, to be a farmer or work in an office?
2 Would you prefer to stay at home all your life or travel to other countries?
3 Which would you prefer, to fly to America or go by sea?
4 Would you prefer to go to a university or start work when you leave school?
5 If you went to London, which would you prefer, to stay with an English family or live in a hotel?
6 Would you prefer to finish this exercise in class or at home?
7 If you owed me some money, would you prefer to pay now or wait until the end of the month?
8 If there was another war, which would you prefer to join, the Army or the Air Force?
9 Would you prefer to have a reading lesson tomorrow or write a composition?
10 Which would you prefer, to have a sandwich for lunch tomorrow or go to a restaurant?
11 If there was a holiday tomorrow, would you prefer to play tennis or go for a bicycle ride?
12 If you were a teacher, which would you prefer, to teach in a secondary or in a primary school?

(c) Use the following words to form 2 questions, and answer them in this way:

Example : do go for a walk watch television
Question 1 : Which would you rather do, go for a walk or watch television?

Notice the comma after *do*. When the question is said, there is a short pause.

Question 2 : Would you rather go for a walk or watch television?
Answer : I'd rather watch television than go for a walk.

or

I'd rather go for a walk than watch television.

Example : play football basket-ball
Question 1 : Which would you rather play, football or basket-ball?
Question 2 : Would you rather play football or basket-ball?
Answer : I'd rather play football than basket-ball (*or* basket-ball than football).

Notice that the Part 1 verb *play* is not repeated.

1	do	stay in bed until nine every day	get up early
2	have	coffee for breakfast	tea
3	do	have lunch at home	at school
4	see	a film	a play
5	do	work abroad	in your own country
6	be	rich and foolish	poor and clever
7	study	foreign languages	mathematics
8	do	drive your own car	have a chauffeur
9	be	a dentist	doctor
10	break	an arm	a leg
11	have	chicken for lunch tomorrow	fish
12	do	wear a raincoat	carry an umbrella
13	do	walk to school	take a bus
14	have	a motor bicycle	a car
15	be	tall	short
16	have	a wrist watch	a pocket watch
17	read	detective novels	books about politics

18	have	a lot of money	a lot of friends
19	do	sit at the back	at the front of the class
20	have	a holiday in the summer	in the winter
21	be	dead	in prison
22	have	a flat in the city	a house in the country
23	play	the piano	the violin
24	be	a teacher	a student

(b) *could*

Read these questions:

> Can you tell me the right time?
> Could you tell me the right time?
> Can I borrow your dictionary?
> Could I borrow your dictionary?

All are present questions, whether *can* or *could* is used; when *could* is used, it has no past meaning. The questions beginning with *could* are more polite; the speaker is making himself 'smaller', which is a polite thing to do.

Exercise 5

Add to each of the following sentences a polite question. The words in brackets are to help you, for example:

> I don't know where he lives. (address)
> Could you give me his address?

Begin your questions: Could you ——

1 I can't hear you very well. (more loudly)
2 I've left my money at home. (lend)
3 The film begins at six o'clock. (meet)
4 I don't understand this word. (meaning)
5 I want to go to the post office. (way to)
6 I don't want a cheque. (cash)

Begin your questions: Could I ——

7 My uncle is coming this afternoon. (home early)
8 I'm still thirsty. (another cup of)
9 I can't see. (near the blackboard)
10 I can't finish the work today. (tomorrow)
11 I can't find my pen. (yours)
12 It's too cold to have a cold bath. (a hot)

(c) *might*

Read these sentences:

> Where are you going for your holiday next summer?
> I may go to Italy.
> I might go to Italy.

might has no past meaning here. Both *may go* and *might go* mean: perhaps I shall go; it is possible that I shall go; but *might* expresses more doubt than *may*.

Exercise 6

Add a sentence using *might* to each of the following. The words in brackets are to help you, for example:

I can't go to the cinema this evening. (tomorrow)
Sentence : I *might* go tomorrow.

1 I'm sure he's not twenty-one yet. (twenty)
2 Don't drive so fast. (an accident)
3 Why don't you buy a lottery ticket? (a lot of money)
4 Take an umbrella with you. (rain)
5 The little boy shouldn't play with that knife. (cut)
6 Are you going to the post office? (some stamps)
7 I can't have more than a week's holiday this year. (next year)
8 I don't think he's French. (Italian)
9 Why don't you ask your father? (more pocket-money)
10 Have you lost your keys? (find)

11 Don't leave your books on your desks when you go out of the classroom. (Someone)

12 Why doesn't he apply for a job with an oil company? (get)

5 Finally, let us see how to express a past wish. Here are some sentences from Section 1 of this chapter, and underneath each a sentence expressing the same wish in the past:

(a) I wish I knew how to drive a car.
I wish I *had known* how to drive a car in 1955 (a past time).

(b) I wish today was a holiday.
I wish yesterday (a past time) *had been* a holiday.

(c) I wish I could travel round the world.
I wish I *could have travelled* round the world when I was a young man. (The speaker is not young, so he is speaking about the past.)

The past wish is expressed by a Past Perfect tense (had known, had been), or by a Perfect Conditional tense (could have travelled).

Exercise 7

Add to each of the following a sentence, using either a Past Perfect or a Perfect Conditional tense after beginning: I wish——

Example: I didn't understand what he said yesterday.
Answer : I wish I *had understood* what he said yesterday.

Example: I made careless mistakes in the last dictation.
Answer : I wish I *hadn't made* careless mistakes in the last dictation.

Example: My father couldn't find a house near the school.
Answer : I wish my father *could have found* a house near the school.

The words in brackets will help you to form your sentences.

1 The shoes I bought last month are too small for me. (a bigger pair)

2 I sat at the back of the hall, and couldn't hear the Minister's speech very well. (every word)

3 He was a very good teacher, but he left this school two years ago.

4 I was late this morning; I didn't wake up until eight o'clock. (earlier)
5 There were no taxis, so I had to walk from the station. (find)
6 I went to bed very late last night, and I'm half-asleep this morning. (so late)
7 Mr. Brown said, "I was lazy and wasted my time when I was at school." (harder)
8 I could only answer three of the questions in the last examination. (all of them)
9 I think the fish I ate last night was bad.
10 My father gave me some good advice, but I didn't take it. (his advice)
11 One of my friends went to Beirut for a holiday last summer, but I couldn't go. (with him)
12 I gave my dictionary to my sister, and now I want it. (to her)
13 The purse was lying on the pavement, but I didn't see it.
14 There was so much noise in the streets last night that I couldn't sleep well. (better)
15 I lent him £5 six months ago, and he hasn't paid me back yet. (any money)
16 The old man said, "I had to leave school when I was fifteen; I couldn't go to a university."
17 I couldn't mend my bicycle; I had to take it to a shop. (myself)
18 There was a very good film on last week, but I didn't see it.
19 We went for a picnic yesterday, but it rained all the time. (so hard)
20 The poor man asked me to help him, but I could only give him a shilling. (more)

Observation 10

Sentences from Exercises 1, 2, or 3 of Chapter 10

Is it right or wrong to put the article *a* in the spaces?

1 He won't get the letter in ——— time.
2 Don't throw ——— rubbish on the floor.
3 I haven't had ——— haircut for over a month, and my hair is very long.

Past Forms, but not Past Time 111

4 I live ——— long way from the school.
5 He has ——— very bad eyesight.
6 I wrote to him ——— fortnight ago, but he hasn't answered my letter yet.
7 It isn't ——— time to go home.
8 We've played ten football matches this year, but we haven't won ——— single game.
9 The poor man has been out of ——— work for a year.
10 My friend can't find ——— good job.

Put the adverbs between brackets in correct positions in the sentences:

1 She's seven years old, but she hasn't started school. (nearly, yet)
2 He drives too fast. (always)
3 The house is too big for them. (much)
4 He's fourteen years old and he wears short trousers. (still)
5 I don't speak English. (fluently)
6 It's 9 a.m. and Jack is in bed. (still)

Sentences from Exercises 4 and 7 only

Which is the correct preposition to put in each space, *at* or *in*?

1 I sat ——— the back of the hall, and couldn't hear the Minister's speech very well.
2 Would you prefer to finish this exercise ——— class or ——— home.
3 Don't park your car ——— front of my gate.
4 Which would you rather have, a flat ——— the city or a house ——— the country?
5 Mr. Brown said, "I was lazy and wasted my time when I was ——— school."
6 There was so much noise ——— the streets last night that I couldn't sleep well.

Is it correct to use the Singular or the Plural word of each pair between brackets?

1 Would you prefer to study foreign (language, languages) or mathematics?
2 The shoes I bought last month (is, are) too small for me.

3 My father gave me some good advice, but I didn't take (it, them).
4 Would you prefer to stay at home all your life or travel to other (country, countries)?
5 There (was, were) no taxis, so I had to walk from the station.
6 Don't make so much (noise, noises).
7 One of my (friend, friends) went to Beirut for a holiday last summer, but I couldn't go.

11 Verb-Nouns

1 Compare these pairs of sentences:

> *Teaching* is hard work.
> Mr. White has been *teaching* English for ten years.

Teaching is the Subject of the first sentence; it is used as a noun, and can be called a verb-noun. (It is called in other grammar books a verbal noun, or gerund.)

In the second sentence, *teaching* is a Present Participle, a part of the Present Perfect Continuous tense *has been teaching*.

> The teacher said, "Don't ask questions yet. I haven't finished *speaking*."
> Children shouldn't interrupt while their parents are *speaking*.

In the first sentence, *speaking* is a verb-noun, the Object of the verb *haven't finished*. In the second sentence, it is a Present Participle, part of the Present Continuous tense *are speaking*.

> He tore up the letter after *reading* it.
> I was *reading* the newspaper when the front door bell rang.

The old grammar books gave this rule: A preposition governs a noun. It also 'governs' a verb-noun, and in the first sentence, *reading* is a verb-noun, 'governed' by the preposition *after*. In the second sentence, *reading* is a Present Participle, part of the Past Continuous tense *was reading*.

2 There are verbs which can take EITHER a verb-noun OR a *to*-stem as Object, with no change of meaning, for example:

> When did you begin *learning* English?
> or
> When did you begin *to learn* English?
>
> I like *going* to the cinema occasionally.
> or
> I like *to go* to the cinema occasionally.

These verbs can take a verb-noun OR a *to*-stem as Object:

begin, continue, hate, intend, like, dislike, love, prefer, start.

There are a few verbs which can take a verb-noun or a *to*-stem as Object, but the meaning is NOT the same. Compare the meanings of these pairs of sentences:

> I remember *meeting* him for the first time ten years ago.
> (I met him in the past, and now I remember.)
> I must remember *to meet* him at the station this evening.
> (I have not met him yet; the meeting is in the future.)
>
> She completely forgot *answering* the letter months ago.
> (She *did* answer the letter, and then she forgot that she had done so.)
> She completely forgot *to answer* the letter.
> (She *didn't* answer the letter, because she had forgotten to.)
>
> He hurt his right hand, so he tried *writing* with his left.
> (He made the experiment of writing with his left hand.)
> The teacher told Ahmad, "Try *to write* more carefully."
> (In this sentence, 'Try' means: Make an attempt.)

Notice also that when a verb-noun follows the verbs *need* or *want*, it has a passive meaning:

> His hair is very long; it needs *cutting*.
> (His hair needs to be cut.)
>
> The grass in the garden is very dry; it wants *watering* badly.
> (The grass wants or needs to be watered.)

Exercise 1

Use verb-nouns OR *to*-stems in place of the verbs in brackets:

1. The windows are very dirty; they need (clean).
2. We read this book in class last year. Do you remember (read) it?
3. He forgot (bring) his exercise-book; he left it at home.
4. If the sun hurts your eyes, why don't you try (wear) dark glasses?
5. Where is my dictionary? Have you forgotten (borrow) it a fortnight ago?

6 The house is old, and it badly wants (paint).
7 He was very forgetful. He never remembered (lock) the garage door when he put the car away.
8 George tried very hard (pass) the examination, but unfortunately he failed.
9 I will always remember (see) Churchill's funeral on television.
10 The floor is covered with dust; it needs (sweep).
11 She often told her little boy, "You must never forget (say) Please and Thank you."
12 Her baby woke up very early in the morning, so she tried (put) him to bed a little later.
13 I remembered to post the letter you gave me, but I didn't remember (buy) any stamps.
14 This shirt is quite clean; it doesn't need (wash) yet.
15 Why are you late again? Have you forgotten (promise) me that you would never be late again?
16 He tried (save) some money before he got married, but he didn't save very much.
17 Don't ask me to pay the bill again. I clearly remember (pay) it a month ago.
18 Her shoes have a hole in them; they want (mend).

3 Some verbs CANNOT take a *to*-stem as Object, but they can take a verb-noun. Examples of such verbs, printed in italics, are given in the following sentences:

(a) Do you *enjoy* listening to gramophone records?
(b) She has *finished* knitting a pullover for her husband.
(c) When I saw a very fat man slip on a banana skin and fall on his back, I *couldn't help* laughing.
(d) Do (Would) you *mind* shutting the window?
(e) He *stopped* smoking a year ago.

There are also phrasal verbs, which can take a verb-noun as Object, but NOT a *to*-stem, for example:

(a) He *went on* talking, although no-one was listening to him.
(b) She *gave up* driving a car after the accident.

Notice also that verb-nouns follow the words printed in italics in these two sentences:

(a) These shoes are so old they *aren't worth* keeping.
(b) It's *no use* crying over spilt milk.

Exercise 2

Use verb-nouns OR *to*-stems in place of the verbs in brackets in the following sentences. First read this list of verbs and phrasal verbs:

(1) avoid	(6) help	(11) carry on
(2) be worth	(7) mind	(12) give up
(3) be no, any use	(8) miss	(13) go on
(4) enjoy	(9) stop	(14) keep on
(5) finish	(10) suggest	(15) leave off
		(16) put off

Now follow these instructions:

(a) If the verb which precedes the verb in brackets is in the above list, use the verb-noun.
(b) If the verb which precedes the verb in brackets is printed in italics, you may use EITHER the verb-noun or the *to*-stem. Both are correct.
(c) All other verbs MUST be followed by *to*-stems.

Example 1: The author hopes (have) a holiday soon, but he must first finish (write) his book.

Answer : The author hopes *to have* a holiday soon, but he must first finish *writing* his book.

The verb *hopes* is not in the above list, and it is not printed in italics, so it is followed by the *to*-stem *to have*. The verb *finish* is No. 5 on the above list, so it is followed by the verb-noun *writing*.

Example 2: It *started* (rain) hard, so it wasn't worth (go) for a picnic.

Answer : It started *raining* (OR *to rain*) hard, so it wasn't worth *going* for a picnic.

The verb *started* is printed in italics, so it may be followed by the verb-noun *raining* or the stem *to rain*. *wasn't worth* is No. 2 on the above list, so it is followed by the verb-noun *going*.

1 He didn't want (lose) any more money, so he gave up (play) cards.
2 His daughter *likes* (listen) to the radio, but he *prefers* (read).
3 He refuses (take) advice from anyone, so it's no use (speak) to him.
4 I *intended* (go) to the cinema yesterday, but my friend told me the film wasn't worth (see).
5 The taxi-driver tried (stop) in time, but he couldn't avoid (hit) the old woman.
6 I *began* (read) the newspaper after breakfast, and I didn't finish (read) it until lunch-time.
7 He offered (buy) my old car, if I didn't mind (wait) a month for the money.
8 The baby *started* (cry) when he woke up, and he went on (cry) all the morning.
9 She *hates* (walk) to work when the buses are full, but she can't afford (take) a taxi.
10 I promised (come) early, but I couldn't help (be) late.
11 The teacher was angry and said, "Stop (ask) silly questions. If you keep on (interrupt) me, I'll send you out of the class."
12 But this pupil *continued* (ask) silly questions, so the teacher decided (punish) him.
13 It left off (rain) and we managed (finish) our game of tennis.
14 I enjoy (look at) television when the programme is worth (watch).
15 Ahmad and his father are going to Europe next summer. Ahmad's father doesn't *like* (fly), so Ahmad suggested (go) by sea.
16 He received the letter a fortnight ago, but he put off (answer) it until yesterday.
17 I hoped (get) to the theatre in time, but unfortunately I missed (see) the first part of the play.
18 The soldier seemed (be) badly wounded, but he carried on (fire) the machine-gun.
19 You may not *like* (tell) lies, but sometimes you can't avoid (tell) them.
20 He pretended (be) rich, but it was no use (pretend); everyone knew he was poor.

4 A preposition 'governs' a verb-noun (see Section 1). Here are some examples of sentences in which prepositions (printed in capital letters) 'govern' verb-nouns:

- (a) You should clean your teeth BEFORE going to bed.
- (b) He tried very hard, and at last he succeeded IN getting a better job.
- (c) I wanted to pay the bus fares, but my friend insisted ON paying.
- (d) The little boy got tired OF playing alone.
- (e) She caught a bad cold, because she isn't used TO sleeping with her windows open.

Note to the teacher: In the last example, *to* is followed by the verb-noun *sleeping* because it is a preposition. There is another construction, which describes a past habit, in this sentence: He *used to play* football, but now he doesn't. Here *to* is NOT a preposition; it forms with *play* a *to*-stem. Pupils are often confused by these two constructions.

Exercise 3

Complete the following sentences sensibly, using verb-nouns after the prepositions printed in capital letters. The words in brackets at the end of some sentences will help you.

Example 1: He went to bed last night WITHOUT ——— (light)
Answer   : He went to bed last night without *turning* off the light.
Example 2: I walked to the station INSTEAD OF ——— (bus)
Answer   : I walked to the station instead of *going* by bus (or *taking* a bus).

A

1 She caught a cold BY ——— (coat)
2 I sent a telegram INSTEAD OF ——— (letter)
3 He still walks five miles a day IN SPITE OF ——— (seventy years old)
4 Everybody congratulated Mahmoud ON ——— (examination)
5 Jack apologised to the teacher FOR ——— (late)
6 The little boy was sick AFTER ——— (a whole box)
7 He's such a truthful man that I don't think he's capable OF ——— (a lie)

Verb-Nouns 119

8 A man should try to save some of his salary INSTEAD OF ―――― (all)
9 I'm sorry if I passed you in the street WITHOUT ――――
10 He is always in debt IN SPITE OF ―――― (salary)
11 She gave the cake to her little brother INSTEAD OF ――――
12 I broke my watch BY ―――― (pavement)

B

1 Students should always read examination questions very carefully BEFORE ――――
2 I missed the train IN SPITE OF ―――― (taxi to)
3 Don't go out in the rain WITHOUT ――――
4 He foolishly tried to cure himself INSTEAD OF ―――― (doctor)
5 People keep cool in a hot climate BY ――――
6 The lazy girl sat watching television INSTEAD OF ―――― (mother)
7 I got tired OF ―――― so I went to bed.
8 Ahmad began to answer the examination questions AFTER ――――
9 Mr. Wilson always teaches the top classes; he isn't used TO ――――
10 He went to work this morning IN SPITE OF ―――― (headache)
11 It is difficult to succeed in life WITHOUT ――――
12 I know it's after midnight, but I'm not going to bed yet. I'm used TO ――――

C

1 He failed the examination BY ―――― (careless)
2 The driver made a mistake and accelerated INSTEAD OF ―――― (the brakes)
3 Please don't enter the room WITHOUT ――――
4 Ahmad can speak English quite well but he's not very good AT ――――
5 She spends very little on clothes IN SPITE OF ――――
6 Doctors and nurses are used TO ―――― (night)
7 I turned off the radio AFTER ――――
8 I wanted to walk, but my friend insisted ON ――――

120 Lesson 11

9 The thieves got into the shop BY ——— (window)
10 He thought for a long time BEFORE ———
11 I listened to the professor's lecture WITHOUT ——— (a word)
12 Some little girls are very fond OF ——— (dolls)

5 Study these sentences and explanations:

>He likes driving a car, but he dislikes *being driven*.

This sentence means: He likes to drive himself, but he doesn't like to be in a car if someone else is driving. This meaning is expressed by using the passive form of the verb-noun: being + Part 3 (driven). This verb-noun is the Object of the verb *dislikes*.

>Most children enjoy *being taken* to the zoo.

being taken (*taken* is Part 3) is another verb-noun in the passive form, the Object of the verb *enjoy*. The meaning of the sentence is clear without saying who take the children to the zoo: their parents, uncles, aunts, friends, or teachers.

>The little boy is very naughty in spite of *being punished* nearly every day.
>The servant complained of *being overworked*.

In these two sentences, the verb-nouns (passive form) *being punished* and *being overworked* follow the prepositions *in spite of* and *of*. We use the passive forms because (1) we are not interested in saying *who* punishes the little boy, and (2) we *know* and do not need to say who overworks the servant.

Exercise 4

Use verb-nouns in the following sentences, formed from the verb stems in brackets. Some must be in the active form (-ing) and others in the passive form (being + Part 3).

1 After the accident, the injured man recovered consciousness in hospital. He remembered (cross) the road, but he didn't remember (knock down).

2 The thief got into the house by (climb) through a window, without (see) by anyone.
3 Ahmad is a much better chess-player than I am, and he was very surprised when I beat him yesterday for the first time. He isn't used to (beat); he is used to (win).
4 This carpet always looks dirty, in spite of (sweep) every day.
5 The little boy was punished for (tell) a lie by (send) to bed without his supper.
6 No-one enjoys (work) like a slave and (underpay).
7 The little girl never gets tired of (ask) her mother questions, but her mother often gets tired of (ask) so many questions.
8 The careless driver had to choose between (pay) a fine of £50 or (send) to prison for a month.
9 I always treat people politely and I insist on (treat) politely.
10 Some workmen dislike (pay) by cheque; they prefer to have cash.
11 Jack doesn't like boxing. I don't know if he is afraid of (hurt) his opponent or of (hurt) himself.
12 The tourist complained of (give) a very small bedroom at the back of the hotel.
13 The prisoner who escaped was only free for a few hours before (catch).
14 The little girl didn't go near the dog; she was afraid of (bite).
15 The young man wasn't satisfied, in spite of (get) a better job and (give) a higher salary.

6 Study the following:

I can't understand the article in this newspaper on foreign politics in spite of *having read* it twice.
The fisherman went home soon after sunset without *having caught* a single fish.

having read and *having caught* are Perfect verb-nouns, used after the prepositions *in spite of* and *without*. If these two sentences are broken up, they become:

I can't understand this article. I *have read* it twice.
The fisherman went home soon after sunset. He *hadn't caught* a single fish.

We now see the reason for using Perfect verb-nouns: because Present or Past Perfect tenses (have read, hadn't caught) are the correct tenses to use in the broken-up sentences.

> The football team has played ten matches this season without *having been beaten* once.
> The watch was still going in spite of *having been dropped* on a stone floor.

having been beaten and *having been dropped* are Perfect verb-nouns in the passive form. The reason for using them is the same: if the sentences were broken up, we should use Perfect tenses:

> The football team has played ten matches. It *hasn't been beaten* once.
> The watch was still going. It *had been dropped* on a stone floor.

The formation of Perfect verb-nouns is:

Active: having + Part 3
Passive: having been + Part 3

Exercise 5

Use Perfect verb-nouns (active OR passive form – your sense will tell you which is the right form), made from the verb-stems in brackets.

1 I am still thirsty in spite of (drink) four cups of tea.
2 He didn't return the book he had borrowed after (promise) to do so.
3 The workmen got tired of waiting and went home without (pay).
4 She didn't get out of bed until ten o'clock in spite of (wake up) at seven.
5 He died penniless (without a penny) at the age of fifty, in spite of (leave) £20,000 by his father.
6 They lived in a small town for ten years and then moved without (make) friends with any of their neighbours.
7 The boy was drowned bathing in the river after (tell) many times that it was dangerous to bathe there.
8 I think he was foolish to buy a car before (learn) how to drive it.

9 She's a rather ignorant woman in spite of (educate) at one of the best girls' schools in England.
10 The old soldier remembered with pride all his life (invite) to the Palace when he was a young man.
11 He went to bed at 9 p.m. in spite of (sleep) all the afternoon.
12 The little girl isn't afraid of dogs in spite of (bite) twice.
13 He was taken to hospital unconscious after the accident. He died in hospital without (recover) consciousness.
14 He can still play a good game of tennis in spite of (lose) a leg in the last war.
15 The old lady never forgot (frighten) by her nurse when she was a little girl.
16 The boy was very hungry at eleven o'clock in spite of (eat) a big breakfast two hours earlier.
17 When he got home from the hospital, he wrote a letter in which he complained of (give) the wrong medicine.
18 The old man had very little to live on, in spite of (work) hard all his life.
19 The baby went to sleep a few minutes after (feed).
20 Mary was chosen a year ago to act in the school play. She was very pleased at (choose).

7 Notice the words printed in italics in these sentences:

(a) He told his son, "It's no use *my* giving you advice if you never take it."
(b) Do you remember *me* telling you not to be late again.
(c) I'm not very friendly with Henry, so I was surprised by *his* asking me to dinner.
(d) The doctor insisted on *him* staying another week in hospital.

The 4 sentences are correct English, but in (a) and (c) Possessive adjectives *my* and *his* are used before the verb-nouns *giving* and *asking*; in (b) and (d) Object pronouns *me* and *him* are used before the verb-nouns *telling* and *staying*.

It is impossible to give rules about the use of Possessive adjectives or Object pronouns before verb-nouns. It can only be said that Possessive adjectives are more 'literary', while Object pronouns are more common in spoken English, and are probably becoming more common in writing also.

Now look at these sentences:

(a) He doesn't mind his *daughter* going to the cinema once a week.

(b) Mary again wrote in pencil, in spite of the *teacher* having told her time after time to write in ink.

(c) The thieves broke into the shop without *anyone* seeing them.

(d) It is difficult to stop *George* talking once he begins.

The Possessive form (his daughter's, the teacher's etc.) is so rarely used before verb-nouns that the student is advised NOT to use it.

Exercise 6

Write the following sentences again, using verb-nouns.

Example 1: I told you that the watch cost £25.
        Have you forgotten ———
Answer : Have you forgotten *me* (or *my*) *telling* you that the watch cost £25?

Example 2: He allows his son to drive his car.
        He doesn't mind ———
Answer : He doesn't mind his *son driving* his car.

1. The children are making such a noise.
   Can't you stop ———?

2. No-one will listen if they complain.
   It's no use ———

3. Pupils must write their corrections carefully.
   The teacher insists on ———

4. Mohamed got his doctor's degree at London University.
   Everyone congratulated his father on ———

5. No-one helped her with her homework.
   She did her homework without ———

6. I wish people wouldn't smoke in cinemas.
   I don't like ———

7. He got my letter although I had addressed it wrongly.
   He got my letter in spite of ———

Verb-Nouns 125

  8 I beat him at tennis, and he wasn't pleased at all.
    He hated ———

  9 Did you give me back the book I lent you?
    I can't remember ———

10 She was afraid that the baby would fall out of bed.
    She was afraid of ———

11 The old lady said I could open the window.
    She didn't mind ———

12 The manager had given him a much higher salary, but the clerk wasn't satisfied.
    The clerk wasn't satisfied in spite of ———

13 I'm sure he asked you not to phone after 11 p.m.
    Have you forgotten ———?

14 He doesn't believe that a boy of twelve should have too much pocket-money.
    He doesn't believe in ———

15 My father doesn't like me to stay out late at night.
    He doesn't like ———

Observation 11

Sentences from any of the exercises in Chapter 11 except No. 3

Of each 2 words in brackets, which is the right one?

1 The boy was drowned bathing in the river after having been told many times that it was dangerous to (bath, bathe) there.

2 The floor is covered with (dust, dusty); it needs sweeping.

3 The little boy was punished for (saying, telling) a lie by being sent to bed without his supper.

4 I (beat, won) him at tennis, and he wasn't pleased at all.

5 I hoped to get to the theatre in time, but unfortunately I (lost, missed) seeing the first part of the play.

6 After the accident, the injured man recovered (conscious, consciousness) in hospital.

7 I think he was (fool, foolish) to buy a car before having learnt how to drive it.

8 He forgot to bring his exercise-book; he (forgot, left) it at home.

9 The old soldier remembered with (pride, proud) all his life having been invited to the Palace when he was a young man.

10 He didn't return the book he had borrowed after having promised to do (it, so).

Is it right or wrong to put the article *the* in the spaces?

1 He didn't want to lose any more money, so he gave up playing —— cards.

2 He died penniless at —— age of fifty, in spite of having been left £20,000 by his father.

3 His daughter likes to listen to —— radio, but he prefers reading.

4 When he got home from the hospital, he wrote a letter in which he complained of having been given —— wrong medicine.

5 I began reading the paper after breakfast, and I didn't finish reading it until —— lunch-time.

6 We read this book in —— class last year. Do you remember reading it?

7 He offered to buy my old car, if I didn't mind waiting a month for —— money.

8 I always treat —— people politely and I insist on being treated politely.